W9-BMK-017

LOST AND FOUND

The Asian American Experience

*Series Editor*
Roger Daniels

*A list of books in the series appears at the end of this book.*

# LOST AND FOUND

## Reclaiming the Japanese American Incarceration

Karen L. Ishizuka

Forewords by
John Kuo Wei Tchen
and Roger Daniels

University of Illinois Press
Urbana and Chicago

Library of Congress Cataloging-in-Publication Data
Ishizuka, Karen L.
Lost and found : reclaiming the Japanese American
incarceration / Karen L. Ishizuka ; foreword by John Kuo Wei Tchen.
p.  cm. — (The Asian American experience)
Catalog of an exhibition held at the Japanese American
National Museum in Los Angeles, Calif.
Includes bibliographical references and index.
ISBN-13: 978-0-252-03130-4 (cloth : alk. paper)
ISBN-10: 0-252-03130-X (cloth : alk. paper)
ISBN-13: 978-0-252-07372-4 (pbk. : alk. paper)
ISBN-10: 0-252-07372-X (pbk. : alk. paper)
1. Japanese Americans—Evacuation and relocation,
1942–1945—Exhibitions. 2. World War, 1939–1945—Japanese
Americans—Exhibitions. I. Japanese American National
Museum (Los Angeles, Calif.)
II. Title. III. Series.
D769.8.A6I78      2006
940.53'1773—dc22      2006003052

# Contents

# Foreword

John Kuo Wei Tchen

> Let America be America again.
> The land that never has been yet.
> And yet must be.
> —Langston Hughes

*Lost and Found: Reclaiming the Japanese American Incarceration* embodies the spirit of a successful exhibition called America's Concentration Camps: Remembering the Japanese American Experience, produced by the Japanese American National Museum and expertly curated by Karen L. Ishizuka. The exhibition and now this book—which incorporates critical post-exhibit insights of the curator—successfully integrate scholarship and storytelling. The volume delivers an intelligent and powerful interactive reclamation of the concentration camp experience, a reclamation that transforms traumatic scars, unspoken grief, and haunted memories into a testament of recognition, voicing, healing, reunion, and reconciliation. Capturing the process by which those who were unjustly imprisoned reclaimed their experience on their own terms, it tells how they also "Let America be America again. / The land," as the poet intones, "that never has been yet. / And yet must be."

I had the good fortune of visiting the exhibition on its opening weekend. I joined thousands of former camp inmates, their families, friends, and others on a painful yet necessary journey to relive the insult of being falsely assumed to be an enemy by one's own country. Everyday objects and photos were placed in a historical context that was informed by the best scholarship on the camps, a framework that helped make sense of a senseless eviction, incarceration, and dispossession. Fortified by her advisors, Ishizuka insisted on reexamining such terms as "concentration camps" and "inmates," which was critical to the transformative process. She was able to piece together—to re-member—a racially scapegoated community's shattered memories and self-understanding.

More than just creating an effective exhibition, Ishizuka curated a safe space where members of the community itself became curators in telling and interpreting their own history. *Lost and Found* is an excellent realization of what I consider "dialogue-driven" public history, history told in concert with the people the history is about. Rather than a single authoritative stance, dialogue-driven knowledge production assumes a meaningful give-and-take with community members and, in my experience, results in more rigorous and accountable scholarship than cloistered academic work.

The exhibition was highly participatory—from the opening orientation tables to the memory books to the separate camp islands through the public programming. There was a hushed intensity among the visitors, a sacred quality to the way they stood and moved through this landscape of sounds, images, and memories. Recollections were being shared, generations were talking and listening across chasms of time, and everyone was carefully and systematically reading, watching, and reflecting. The Los Angeles installation and then the traveling versions at Ellis Island, Atlanta, San Francisco, and Little Rock sparked numerous reunions among former inmates and their families, and also with other friends and families, both Japanese American and of other ethnicities. The exhibition itself became an interactive means by which further documentation, storytelling, and collections were cultivated, gathered, and valued. Each step of the way was deliberately curated to maximize interaction, meaningful participation, and analytic reexamination.

This was the precious, rare work of reclaiming a past by opening up safe, reflexive space in the present. It created at once a private personal moment of reflection and a communal group encounter that effectively served as a debriefing, a decompression. For many, it was the first time they had truly experienced this since they left the camps. To publicly reclaim the dislocation and trauma was to privately engage in a healing process, for the survivors and for those who care about social justice. The past recalled from the vantage point of this entrusted moment helped them to reintegrate their lives and find their place in this country anew. That reclamation—the collective storymaking and storytelling that began in the exhibition—is now conveyed in this book. It captures the dialogic role the exhibition played in building a collective memory and an accurate record of an experience kept secret for too long. It achieves what the historian Michael H. Frisch calls "a shared authority" between the "experts" and those whose experiences are represented (Frisch, *A Shared Authority* [Albany: State University of New York Press, 1990]).

*Lost and Found* is a wholly original work. It has no true counterpart. Perhaps it is comparable to Allon Schoener's *Harlem on My Mind*, a companion to the 1969 blockbuster exhibit of the same title, but to my way of thinking it is much better, both historically and in its quality of analysis. It has some similarities to a series of excellent books published by the New Press. Lucy Lippard edited a volume called *Partial Recall* (1993) with photographs that reclaimed the images of native peoples and essays that were at once highly personal and rehistoricizing. So too the work of Deborah Willis in *Picturing Us: African American Identity in Photography* (1994). Books on Joseph Kosuth's installation *The Play of the Unmentionable* (1992) at the Brooklyn Museum and Fred Wilson's exhibition Mining the Museum (1994) at the Maryland Historical Society in Baltimore dramatically illustrate how exhibits can challenge standard curatorial practices and provoke audiences into new critical spaces. Yet, none of these book versions of exhibitions has so successfully blended excellent historical scholarship and profound audience interaction as *Lost and Found.*

*Lost and Found* reaches out beyond the generations who directly experienced the camps' impact. It is written in a clear, straightforward manner that speaks to a broad public beyond the Japanese American community. It is accessible, full of vivid detail, and told with great vitality. I find the stories absolutely fresh, opening up many new angles of understanding. This dialogic work is not simply about reexamining a historic wrong. It is about challenging how deception and knowledge are produced and circulated. It is a powerful example of tackling a most difficult subject for U.S. citizens in a fully open and engaging manner. Confident in the many truths it presents, Ishizuka has crafted this book for all who care about social justice and human rights.

Vigilante Americanism such as the scapegoating of Japanese Americans during World War II must be challenged and replaced with a truly patriotic ethic of Americanism "for all." How can "we, the people," unite to build a just and equitable future if we are still torn by wrongs of the past? De facto citizens must be publicly confirmed as full Americans whose rights cannot be violated. How patriotic is the so-called Patriot Act passed in the aftermath of 9/11? Truth and frank dialogue must be part and parcel to the way we practice democracy. *Lost and Found* shows that if it can be done in this one instance, it can also be done on issues of enslavement, dispossession, and racial profiling. We need to define and redefine American values of justice and equity. This book is both a celebration of a job exquisitely done and a call to Americans to come together again to work for more historical justice in a nation that promises so much.

# Foreword

Roger Daniels

The incarceration of more than 120,000 persons, some 70 percent of them native-born United States citizens, between 1942 and 1946, was and remains the central event of Japanese American history. For decades after the event, most community members spoke very little about it; some parents did not even tell children born in those years that their nativity had taken place in a concentration camp. By the 1970s, in a nation that was being changed by the civil rights movement and the misbegotten war in Vietnam, the Japanese American community, slowly and painfully, began to come to grips with its past. The long struggle for redress, capped by the passage of the Civil Rights Act of 1988, in which the federal government made an unprecedented apology for its wartime violations of the rights of both citizens and resident aliens and awarded $20,000 each to more than 80,000 survivors, was surely the key process in the communal change of attitude. As one newly activist Nisei woman said to me during a fiftieth anniversary commemoration in 1992, involvement in the redress movement "loosened our tongues."

In 1984, while the redress struggle was still joined, some community leaders incorporated the Japanese American National Museum as a nonprofit institution; eight years later it opened its doors in Los Angeles, in Little Tokyo, sited in the former Nishi Hongwanji Buddhist Temple, which had been one of the places at which the federal government ordered Japanese Americans to assemble for shipment to a concentration camp in 1942. Created as part of the community reorientation associated with redress, the museum has become a vital part of the process by which the community came to grips with its past. An early, sensitive review by David K. Yoo, entitled "Captivating Memories: Museology, Concentration Camps, and Japanese American History," appeared in the *American Quarterly* (48, no. 4 [1996]: 680–99).

Karen L. Ishizuka was a key staff member for the first fifteen years of the museum's existence. She helped establish the museum's commitment to community as well as its Photographic and Moving Image Archive and Media Arts Center. During her tenure she produced many award-winning films and curated a major exhibition, America's Concentration Camps: Remembering the Japanese American Experience. As she shows in the present volume, although the museum was and is staffed by a skilled group of professionals, in a sense the community was "curator" as thousands of individuals in dozens of ways were able to help recreate the community's past.

She has given us an insider's nuanced account of the creation of America's Concentration Camps and tells the story of its sometimes conflicted history as a traveling exhibition. The book is both history and memory, but without the superfluous postmodern baggage that is so trendy today. It is punctuated with dozens of wonderful concrete details. Although I have been lecturing and writing about the incarceration for almost fifty years, I never thought about how many barracks there must have been. Ishizuka tells us that 2,276 barracks were identified by individual exhibition visitors as their particular "residences." To me, one of the most fascinating things about this account is the richness of interactive experiences that Ishizuka is able to relate. She gives example after example of the ways individuals came to understand how to participate in their own history. Her book illustrates how the museum and community members educated one another.

I viewed the exhibit in two very different contexts. In Los Angeles, early in the exhibit's life, my fellow viewers were largely former camp residents and their families. In Little Rock, in 2004 most of my fellow viewers were surviving prisoners of Arkansas's two camps, Jerome and Rohwer, returning to the state for the first time since their release. But we were joined by native Arkansans who were just discovering some of the darker aspects of their state's history. Reading *Lost and Found: Reclaiming the Japanese American Incarceration* represents a third kind of visit, for its unique insights supplement what I had previously experienced. Whether one has seen the exhibit before or encounters it here for the first time, Ishizuka's book will enhance significantly each reader's awareness of the existential aspects of an American tragedy.

# Preface

This book tells the life history of the exhibition America's Concentration Camps: Remembering the Japanese American Experience. From its conception and the development of its exhibition strategy and design, to its manifestation that brought history alive, to the unexpected and enlightening stories that walked in the door, and the discoveries of recovery that continued to be made after its doors were closed, the show took on a life of its own. As it traveled to New York, Atlanta, San Francisco, and Little Rock in the ensuing ten years, like every life, it encompassed precious moments, embraced remarkable people, and unveiled significant lessons that, as its curator, I feel are worth passing on.

The exhibition opened at the Japanese American National Museum in Los Angeles in November 1994 with the usual array of artifacts, text panels, photographs, and displays. However as the historian Jon Wiener wrote in *The Nation* (May 15, 1995, 694), "'America's Concentration Camps: Remembering the Japanese American Experience' is not the usual history exhibit." What began as a standard exhibition curated and designed by a professional team of museum curators, designers, and academic consultants became the backdrop for a much more engaging and potent exhibition that not only evolved but, in essence, was curated over time by the visitors themselves. By offering camp survivors simple opportunities for interactivity—signing their names and camp addresses in camp registries, placing their barracks on camp maps, adding their Polaroid portraits and memories to camp albums—the exhibition invited traditionally passive museum goers to dynamically alter and enhance a carefully considered but nonetheless static display. By engaging the audience in the presentation of its own history within the context of the exhibition, the show enabled visitors not only to recover history but to recover from it as well.

*Lost and Found: Reclaiming the Japanese American Incarceration* presents this process of reclamation, which would otherwise be ephemeral. It is not meant to be a textbook on the episode or a scholarly treatise on any of its many aspects. It contemplates the questions of what becomes history, and from whose point of view. It asks how people can be encouraged to face dark moments and come away even stronger. It considers why we should remember when many would just as soon forget.

It also favors storytelling over analysis, and attempts to present both in a framework of reflectivity. I had five grandparents, one father, two mothers, twenty-five aunts and uncles, and one cousin who had been in camp. I have included many of their images and stories in this book to emphasize that history happens to, and is made by, ordinary people.

My generation was brought up by a community who had been falsely accused and punished for a crime they did not commit. Like many other Sansei (third-generation Japanese Americans), I was not in camp, but I inherited its indignity. When I accepted the responsibility of curating the exhibition, I had already spent a lifetime trying to comprehend and reconcile this part of my history. I wrote a master's thesis on the effects of the incarceration on identity in 1970, a play for the redress and reparations movement in 1981, and a film on the long-term psychological impact of the camps in 1985. As a curator, my mandate from the Japanese American National Museum was to produce an introductory exhibition on camp to a broad audience. However, as a Sansei, my responsibility was to also make it meaningful to my parents, aunts, uncles, and other camp survivors whose lives had such an impact on my own.

Throughout the book I found myself interchanging pronouns and who they signified. I used "they" to acknowledge those who were actually in camp. Yet sometimes I found myself using "we," as participants in a collective Japanese American experience. At other times, however, "we" referred to "we the people," Americans as a whole. And at yet other times, "we" meant all of us, humankind in general, whose duty it is to learn from the past, distinguish truth from propaganda, and sum-

The author's grandmother Yoshiko Tanaka in the Manzanar concentration camp, California, ca. 1943. Courtesy of George Ishizuka.

The author's aunt and uncle, Setsuko (Nishi) and Elmer Uchida, and her cousin, Randy Uchida, are shown in Manzanar, ca. 1944. Collection of the Japanese American National Museum (hereafter, JANM), gift of Mary S. Ishizuka (98.128.175).

Shown left to right, the author's grandfather Momota Okura, aunt Etsuko, uncle Susumu, grandmother Fuyu, aunt Shizuko, and uncle Tsuyoshi in the Jerome concentration camp, Arkansas, ca. 1944. Courtesy of Frances Okura (NRC 1998.230.1).

mon the conviction to stand our ground. While at first I attempted to correct this mixing of pronouns, I realized that this blurring of third and first person expresses the multiplicity of identity and ownership, the coalition of audience and author, community as curator.

This book tells about process and participation, yet it also participates in the very process it describes. It is part of a multigenerational, multidisciplinary process to understand, uncover, and ultimately prevent America's concentration camps from ever happening again.

# Acknowledgments

One of the great ironies of publication has to be that readers and authors attend to a book's acknowledgments in inverse proportion to one another. The readers perform an obligatory scanning—except for those looking for their own names—often bypassing the litany entirely. The author, on the other hand, sincerely agonizes over how to recognize and adequately thank the universe of those who enabled the book to be, ultimately feeling inadequate in the undertaking. With profound apologies to those I will inevitably omit, I offer the following, sparing the superlatives and beseeching your indulgence.

First and foremost my gratitude goes to Roger Daniels, the editor of this series. Like thousands of others, I first knew of him as a renowned and formidable historian for his pioneering research and writing. He helped establish and legitimize Asian American studies, filling large cracks in the melting pot as he went. In the development of the exhibition upon which this book is based, he was my foremost academic advisor and one of three people (the others were Michi Weglyn and Aiko Herzig-Yoshinaga) with whom I had almost weekly correspondence. In the publication of a book, not often is an author fortunate enough to have a series editor who is also an expert in her subject matter. In addition to overseeing the project, Roger in essence acted as my chief consultant, upon whom I relied for historical accuracy and discussions regarding nuance. At the University of Illinois Press, my acquisitions editor, Laurie Matheson, did a masterful job of shepherding me through the many stages of publication. And in the chaos of creative expression where I often found words inadequate, my copy editor, Carol Betts, provided a new appreciation for how precise the written word can be.

I prevailed upon a few selected colleagues, friends, and family members—people whose backgrounds are varied, whose opinions I respected, and whose honesty I counted upon—to read the entire manuscript at various incarnations. Robert Dawidoff, a historian; Jim Hirabayashi, an anthropologist; Lloyd Inui, a political scientist; and Kathy Ishizuka, a writer, read early renditions and provided cogent suggestions. Thai Binh Checel, an educator; Bruce Iwasaki, an attorney; and John Kuo Wei Tchen, a historian, provided close readings of the final manuscript from diverse perspectives that ultimately smoothed its rough spots and sharpened its focus.

At the Japanese American National Museum there are countless staff and volunteers, past and present, without whose assistance I would still be toiling. Yoko Okunishi and Susan Fukushima spent hours finding and clearing all the images from the museum's collection. I am extremely appreciative of their good work and good spirit. Norman Sugimoto took many of the photographs and was always gracious and accommodating. Traci Kato-Kiriyama, Alison Kochiyama, Masaki Miyagawa, Grace Murakami, Cris Paschild, Cameron Trowbridge, Kazumi Yoneyama, and others made calls, photocopied, enabled, scanned, researched, and otherwise helped in immeasurable ways. Nancy Araki, Art Hansen, Karin Higa, Irene Hirano, Akemi Kikumura-Yano, and Brian Niiya read and commented on various chapters and drafts.

In the long journey to this point there were others whose expertise may not be evident but whose input was nonetheless appreciated. They include Russell Ferguson, Carolyn See, Hall Smyth, Joe Wood, and especially Qris Yamashita. Again, there are no doubt others whose assistance I am overlooking.

It is said that sentient beings are always surrounded by ten thousand bodhisattvas, bodhisattvas being both celestial entities and anyone who helps move you forward, whether you know it or not. Through their wisdom as well as their ignorance, their encouragement, and especially their criticism, they have led the way and watched my back. I acknowledge and thank them all.

## LOST AND FOUND

# 1 / The Legacy of Camp

August 12, 1994

As I sit here engulfed with the myriad tasks and responsibilities of putting an exhibit together I feel, as I have felt more than once this past year, even more overwhelmed by the strength, determination, pain and suffering of the 120,313 people whose direct experience this is.

Mine is not a singular responsibility. This is not the first effort to present and ponder America's concentration camps, nor hopefully will it be the last. I stand on the shoulders of more people, organizations and efforts than I can name who have conducted research, written memoirs, made films, art, literature and produced exhibits in an effort to better understand the experience.

Mine is, however, a very privileged experience. At this time in history, more than half of those who were incarcerated have already left us. And I am in a special position to cross paths with a few of the remaining before they—and I too—take our leave.

Rather than authorities, we at the museum are catalysts. We seek to join you and ask you to join us in the ongoing process of coming to grips with the incarceration, learning more about its many issues and nuances, and applying its lessons for now and the future.[1]

During World War II, the United States was at war in Europe and the Pacific. Yet, there was a battle on the home front as well. Although the United States was at war with Italy and Germany besides Japan, only Japanese Americans were uprooted en masse from their homes and placed in compounds encircled by barbed wire and surrounded by armed guards in what historians, social commentators, and even the United States government called "concentration camps." By the end of the war, 120,313 Japanese Americans—including both immigrant residents who were not allowed to become naturalized U.S. citizens until 1952 and their children who were born in the United States—had been confined in these camps from a few months to over four years. The camps were located in Arizona, Arkansas, California, Colorado, Idaho, Texas, Utah, and Wyoming. The thousands of American residents and citizens held there were judged without charges, trials, or any manner of due process of law. Although they were incarcerated for allegedly posing a threat to national security, there was no evidence—then or since—to support the accusation. In a country where one is innocent until proven guilty, this was a failure of democracy that has widespread implications for all Americans.

Compounding the injury, the Japanese American community and the American public at large were distanced from the truth by a complex web composed in part of classified information that withheld facts, a resurrected yellow journalism that both reflected and fueled the xenophobia of the times, and government-created euphemisms that were mitigating and misleading. It took a multitude of researchers, historians, and former inmates forty years to make the truth of the matter known. In 1980, the Commission on Wartime Relocation and Internment of Civilians (CWRIC) was established to conduct a comprehensive investigation of the incarceration. After analyzing government documents, reviewing contemporary writings, and hearing directly from former inmates in a series of congressional hearings across the country, the commission reached its official conclusion in 1982, finding that, contrary to what the government said during the 1940s, the incarceration was not justified by military necessity. As the commission's report stated, "The broad historical causes which shaped these decisions were race prejudice, war hysteria and a failure of political leadership. . . . A grave injustice was done to American citizens and resident nationals of Japanese ancestry who, without individual review or any probative evidence against them, were excluded, removed and detained by the United States during World War II."[2] A presidential apology and monetary reparations were issued eight years later.

While many Americans are still not aware such an abrogation of civil rights ever occurred, generations of Americans of Japanese ancestry have struggled and continue to struggle with what they went through and why. The Japanese American National Museum—which we also refer to as the National Museum—was founded in 1985, as its mission statement states, "to promote understanding and appreciation of Amer-

The author (third from left) with the Ralph Applebaum Associates design team (left to right) Ralph Appelbaum, Melanie Ide, and T. Kevin Sayama. Photograph by Robert A. Nakamura.

ica's ethnic and cultural diversity by preserving, interpreting, and sharing the experience of Japanese Americans." While the mission is broad, a primary motivation of the museum's founders was their commitment to educate the general public about the Japanese American experience during World War II.

America's Concentration Camps: Remembering the Japanese American Experience opened at the Japanese American National Museum on November 11, 1994, and closed on October 15, 1995. The exhibition was designed by Ralph Appelbaum Associates, led by Ralph Appelbaum, Melanie Ide, and T. Kevin Sayama. A traveling version was exhibited at the Ellis Island Immigration Museum in New York from April 13, 1998, to January 31, 1999 (which is discussed in chapter 7); the William Breman Museum of Jewish Heritage in Atlanta, Georgia, from August 27 to November 5, 1999; the California Historical Society in San Francisco, from March 21 to June 17, 2000; and the Little Rock Statehouse Convention Center in Arkansas, from September 24 to November 28, 2004.

## Inheriting Camp

For Americans of Japanese ancestry, "camp," as it is commonly referred to, has become central to our collective and individual identities, so much so that our history before and after the camps is often overlooked in comparison. While identity is formed from a complex mix of internal and external factors, ours is particularly shaped by the camp experience. The historians Roy Rosenzweig and David Thelen concluded that in contrast to white Americans, who perceived the past in personal terms, African Americans and American Indians had a collective connection to broadly shared experiences such as slavery, the civil rights movement, and violation of Indian treaties.[3] In a similar way for Japanese Americans, the exclusion and incarceration was a defining episode not only in their history but also in their sense of identity. For example, the questions "Were you in camp?" and "What camp were you in?" inevitably come up in the social ritual of introduction and conversation.

Camp has also become a critical part of the ethnic identity and shared

*All Americans*

The author's father, George Ishizuka (standing, far left), and his brothers Harry Tanaka (front row, second from left), Henry (second row, seated at left), and Frank (top row, center) are shown with friends in Long Beach, California, in 1923, at the height of the anti-Japanese campaign that would result in the cessation of further immigration from Japan the following year. In his album, Ishizuka labeled the photo "All Americans." Collection of JANM, gift of George T. Ishizuka (98.128.2).

history of those of us who were born after the war. Like other Sansei, I grew up hearing time divided into "before the war" and "after the war." "Before the war my folks owned a grocery store; after the war my father became a gardener." "Before the war my mother used to paint; after the war she took in laundry." "Before the war we used to go on family outings; after the war we didn't go anywhere." So we knew about "before" and "after" but hardly anything about the event that had so distinctly divided these memories.

The Nisei, born in the United States and growing up American in the 1910s, 1920s and 1930s, wholeheartedly embraced the lessons of freedom, liberty, equality, and justice they were taught. Their patriotism was even officially recognized by the U.S. government as early as November 1941 when it conducted a secret investigation to assess the loyalty of Japanese Americans in Hawai'i in the event of war with Japan. The Munson Report, which presented the findings of the investigation, indicated that not only were Nisei loyal to the United States, "The Nisei are pathetically eager to show this loyalty." It stated, "They are not Japanese in culture. They are foreigners to Japan. Though American citizens they are not accepted by Americans, largely because they look different and can be easily recognized."[4]

While Nisei experienced the discrimination and unfair treatment to which all racial minorities in the United States are subjected, they never expected to be criminalized by their own government. They had been taught that as American citizens they were protected by the Constitution and the Bill of Rights. When they were summarily imprisoned without due process, the blow left many angry and betrayed and most hurt and confused.

As a result, most former inmates said little about camp to their children. One of my earliest recollections of my parents' mentioning camp was when I gave them a gift of apple butter. Instead of sharing in my delight of what I considered a specialty item, they laughingly explained that in camp, apple butter had been a poor substitute for real butter and they had so much of it they never wanted to eat it again. This kind of culinary association can also work in reverse; my uncle had so much Spam in camp, rumor has it he still has a Spam sandwich for lunch every day.

Many Sansei have similar apple butter and Spam stories, odd examples of times when their parents and relatives would obliquely refer to camp. More often than not, such references would be tempered with disclaimers such as "but why cry over spilled milk," "let bygones be bygones," and "forgive and forget." However, despite the bygones and the spilled milk, we realized that although they did not articulate it, our parents were very much affected by camp. In fact, camp had a lot to do with who they were and how they raised us.

Most children are urged by their parents to do their best. However, for us Sansei, there was an urgency to our parents' exhortations to do well that seemed to transcend our own benefit. Many people of color, especially of our parents' generation, had wearily learned that they had to be twice as good as the next person to prove their worth. As former inmates of America's concentration camps, they found this lesson sharpened by having been imprisoned by their own government because of their race. As heirs to this indignity, we were recruited to be part of their unspoken mission to be 200 percent American. They tacitly believed that sustained model citizenry would provide retroactive evidence that it was "they," meaning but never naming the U.S. government, and not "we" who had been in the wrong. And the Nisei would thereby be absolved of their, which had become "our," humiliation.

As I continued to talk with former inmates about their experiences, I concluded that as a group they knew the most about the incarceration—and the least. On the eve of World War II and during the ensuing upheaval, they were mere children and teenagers who suddenly found themselves with the face of the enemy. They were the ones who watched helplessly as their fathers were whisked away after December 7, 1941. A few months later, Executive Order 9066 was signed by President Franklin D. Roosevelt, mandating their removal and leading to their detention. And they were the ones to help their mothers dispose of all their belongings and decide what precious little they could take to an unknown destination for an unknown period of time. They were the ones who felt the hurt of friends who turned against them and gratitude for those who did not. They were the ones who had to make the best of a bad situation. And yet, many of these same people were still separated from the facts and historical analyses that would allow them finally to understand the history they were a part of but not privy to.

Many former inmates had never read the books and articles that exposed, discussed, and analyzed the political, social, economic, and historical factors, issues, consequences, and implications of the event. I realized, given the government's containment of image and information, that this scholarship is critical to comprehending what transpired. Most of the material had been discovered, researched, and published years after the inmates' release from camp and often during a time when they were more preoccupied with living their present and planning their future than analyzing their past. Yet they needed to know about such facts as the findings of the Munson Report, or that 2,260 Latin Americans of Japanese descent were deported from thirteen countries and imprisoned in the United States to be used as hostages in exchange for American POWs held in Japan,[5] or that the estimated economic loss to the Japanese American community at the time of the forced exclusion was $203 to $251 million.[6] Such knowledge would go a long way in enabling the Nisei to understand that no matter how the government rationalized its actions, and whether or not the Nisei had been able to make the best of it, the government was wrong.

## Semantics of Suppression

One effective method with which the reality of the camp experience has been kept from honest scrutiny is the use of official language to describe it. It is more palatable to talk of "evacuees" instead of prisoners, that they were "relocated" instead of forced from their homes and incarcerated, that they resided in "relocation centers" rather than imprisoned in concentration camps. The earliest known use of the term "concentration camp" with regard to the Japanese American incarceration was by President Franklin D. Roosevelt himself five years before the bombing of Pearl Harbor. In a White House memorandum addressed to the chief of operations, dated August 10, 1936, Roosevelt wrote, "One obvious thought occurs to me—that every Japanese citizen or non-citizen on the Island of Oahu who meets these Japanese ships or has any connection with their officers or men should be secretly but definitely identified and his or her name placed on a special list of those who would be the first to be placed in a concentration camp in the event of trouble."[7]

At the time I was conducting research for the exhibition, professional historians had published this astonishing statement in a few academic books.[8] However, attesting to the community's ability to tell its own story, it deserves mentioning that the document was independently discovered in 1994 by Dave and Margaret Masuoka, volunteers at the Japanese American National Museum. Long retired, with no background in research, they were on vacation in Northern California when they happened upon the West Coast office of the National Archives. Because of their interest in recovering their history, they inquired about documents pertaining to the incarceration and were shocked to find this early statement by none other than the president of the United States. Regarding this memorandum, the historian Greg Robinson writes, "Yet, even without overstating its connection to future events, the memo is significant. . . . It demonstrates the President's willingness to tolerate arbitrary action against Japanese Americans in the name of preserving security and his indifference to the constitutional rights of those citizens and aliens involved."[9]

The term "concentration camp" referring to the mass incarceration of Japanese Americans has since been widely used by scholars, government officials, and the mainstream media. Witness book titles alone: *America's Concentration Camps* (1967), by Allan Bosworth; *Concentration Camps, USA* (1971), by Roger Daniels; *Years of Infamy: The Untold Story of America's Concentration Camps* (1976), by Michi Weglyn; *Keeper of Concentration Camps* (1987), by Richard Drinnon; and *Inside an American Concentration Camp* (1995), by Richard S. Nishimoto and edited by Lane Ryo Hirabayashi. There are many other books that document the use of the term in relation to the World War II incarceration of Japanese Americans.[10]

Historically the term was used both to uphold and to condemn the camps. On December 15, 1941, Congressman John Rankin stated, "I'm for catching every Japanese in America, Alaska, and Hawai'i now and putting them in concentration camps."[11] Two years later, Attorney General Francis Biddle wrote, "The present procedure of keeping loyal American citizens in concentration camps on the basis of race for longer than is absolutely necessary is dangerous and repugnant to the principles of our Government."[12]

Official U.S. government and military documents couched the incarceration in euphemistic terms. The detention orders issued by the U.S. government were called "civilian exclusion orders," in which U.S. citizens of Japanese descent were referred to as "non-aliens."[13] In documents such as *Questions and Answers for Evacuees*, which can be seen in chapter 4, the barbed-wire-enclosed camps were called "relocation centers" and even "pioneer communities with basic housing and protective services provided by the Federal Government."[14] The semantics of suppression masked the gross injustice of the incarceration and shielded America's concentration camps from public examination.

Although the majority of the U.S. Supreme Court justices accepted the euphemistic terminology without examination, Judge Owen J. Roberts on December 18, 1944, boldly stated, "An 'assembly center' was a euphemism for a prison . . . so-called 'relocation centers,' a euphemism for concentration camps."[15] In 1961 Harry S. Truman, the former president, said, "They were concentration camps. They called it relocation but they put them in concentration camps. . . . We were in a state of emergency but it was still the wrong thing to do."[16] Five years later, the former attorney general of the United States, Tom Clark, stated, "I have made a lot of mistakes in my life. . . . One is my part in the evacuation of Japanese in 1942. . . . We picked them up and put them in concentration camps. That's the truth of the matter."[17]

The extensive and persistent use of euphemisms functioned to undermine, demoralize, and gain the cooperation of the victims of the incarceration. Amy Iwasaki Mass, a clinical social worker who spent three years of her childhood in a concentration camp and a lifetime learning to live with it, was one of the speakers for our docent-training program. She pointed out that sometimes it was easier to believe the propaganda than face the truth; she said that former inmates use the defense mechanisms of repression, denial, and rationalization to keep from thinking that their own country had not only failed to protect them but had acted against them.[18]

Another camp survivor, Raymond Okamura, was a key figure in the campaign to repeal the Emergency Detention Act of 1950, which allowed for mass arrests similar to the World War II incarcerations.[19] Okamura called attention to the social and political repercussions of such psychological effects: "One indication of the emotional scars left by the incarceration is the continued use of the government euphemisms by the former prisoners. . . . If this practice persists, no one will be able to testify to the magnitude of the occurrence."[20]

Euphemisms deceived the American and worldwide publics in addition to Americans of Japanese ancestry. With a few notable exceptions, newspapers not only adopted the euphemisms but, reminiscent of the "yellow peril" campaign propagated by the Hearst papers in the early 1900s, used them to fan the flames of war hysteria. An editorial in the *Los Angeles Times* in May 1942 defended the mass exclusion of Japanese Americans by stating that "in wartime the safety of the nation is paramount to the convenience of the individual,"[21] an attitude that has again become prevalent in this country's post-9/11 preoccupation with national security over civil rights. In December 1943, the *Los Angeles Times* published the results of its "Jap Questionnaire." To the loaded question, "Do you favor a constitutional amendment after the war for the deportation of all Japanese from this country, and forbidding further immigration?" the response was 10,598 in favor and 732 opposed. Comments published in the newspaper included, "Banish all Japs from American soil. We can't help it if some are innocent; we will be protecting our country."[22]

During the ethnic awareness movements of the 1960s and 1970s, euphemisms related to the incarceration were exposed, widely discussed, and hotly debated. Similarly, the museum's decision to use the term "concentration camp" did not go unconsidered. Concerns were

Anti-Japanese article from the *Los Angeles Herald Express*, November 13, 1944. Collection of JANM, gift of the American Friends Service Committee (94.122.2B).

**LOS ANGELES EVENING**
# HERALD Express

FRANK F. BARHAM, PUBLISHER

WEDNESDAY, NOVEMBER 15, 1944

## California Does Not Want Japs to Return

### Public Sentiment Strong Against Release of Any Nips to Coast Area

California does not want any Japs ever returned to California.

If Japs come to California, encouraged by the W. R. A. or any other organization, they will do so at their own peril.

The memory of thousands of our finest American boys who have perished at the hands of Japs—the memory of Pearl Harbor—the memory of the treachery of these Japanese who lived here but gave their loyalty to a nation of savages is the reason why we don't want Japs here.

Day after day certain government agencies give out propaganda of a single Jap that has died fighting for the United States of America on some European battle ground.

On that same day a thousand American boys met death and several thousand were wounded, but with no notice, whatever, except in the list of casualties.

The Jap who fought for this country in Europe and his family are entitled to recognition in full by the United States—but if he survives, both himself and his family should live in the east and not in the west, where a Jap is a Jap and we remember dead American boys killed by Japs.

With much secrecy, the War Relocation Authority has suggested that the California State Department of Social Welfare "sound out" sentiment in regard to whether the Japs would be welcome to return.

The suggestion is stupid and out of line.

In other sections of the country the War Relocation Authority has already released many thousands of Japs from internment centers, permitting them to settle in eastern and midwestern states.

The net result of this move has been that the War Relocation Authority has been besieged with protests from such areas—and pleas that they put the Japs back in evacuation centers.

In spite of this the W. R. A. now wants to wish the Japs back on California, Washington and Oregon, states most liable to be under fire if Japan should raid the mainland.

This must not be permitted.

The Army moved the Japs away from the Pacific Coast in the interest of national security. The reasons for this move exist today and will continue to exist.

The Army supports the California public in resisting any move on the part of the War Relocation Authority to give the Japs freedom of movement here.

Californians waste little sympathy on the Japs. They feel that it was a mistake to release any of them from the Tule Lake center.

Let us keep the Japs out forever.

raised. As a national museum, how would this position affect us in terms of governmental and private funding support? Could we afford to be so blatant? In essence, what would people think?

Irene Hirano, president and chief executive of the National Museum and other leaders of the institution met with their counterparts from Jewish organizations such as the Skirball Cultural Center, the American Jewish Committee, and the Simon Wiesenthal Center as well as with representatives from other ethnic organizations.[23] Some Jewish leaders felt the term "concentration camp" had become synonymous with the Holocaust and should therefore be kept within that context. Other Jews insisted that the term "concentration camp" was itself a euphemism for death camp. Leaders of other ethnic institutions reminded us that there have been many concentration camps throughout world history.

Ralph Appelbaum, the exhibition designer, wrote, "The museum will have an opportunity to address and clarify the terminology to the public and discussion is likely to start immediately by virtue of the title alone. . . . By changing the title to something less 'sensitive,' the entire exhibit will soften."[24] James Hirabayashi, chief program advisor to the museum, supplied documentation of his own effort in 1976 to support use of the term "concentration camp" on the historical plaque commemorating the Tule Lake camp in California.[25] And he challenged, "Why did we establish the Japanese American National Museum anyway? To make known Japanese American history from the Japanese American perspective. Then it seems to me, it is up to us to figure out the best way of telling this history and convincing the general public why it is important for us to define this reality as we experienced it."[26]

In the exhibition script, I had originally softened the first reference to the term with the qualifier, "in what has become known as 'America's Concentration Camps.'" When I sent the text to the members of the exhibition advisory committee for their feedback, the historian Roger Daniels retorted, "Why temper it by attaching the qualifier, 'America's' concentration camps—call them what they were: concentration camps!"[27] The writer Michi Weglyn, the attorney and activist Phil Taijitsu Nash, and other members of the advisory committee also provided vast evidential support of the use of the term "concentration camp" by government officials.

We all took into serious consideration the museum's goal not only to educate the public about this little-known chapter of American history but to provide an accurate account from a Japanese American perspective. Nothing about the use of the historically accurate term disparaged or diminished the respect we held for the victims and survivors of the Jewish Holocaust. If any comparisons were to be made it was that we stood with Jews in emphasizing the need for all people to remember and speak out against injustice in order that the horrors of the past are never repeated.

As the discussion continued, our advisors recommended against using the more sanitized term "internment." Roger Daniels, Aiko Herzig-Yoshinaga, and others pointed out that internment is a specific legal process—long recognized by both American and international law—by which selected nationals of enemy nations are placed in confinement.[28] And indeed, many Japanese Americans during World War II were "interned" as enemy aliens (as were Italian Americans and German Americans). The internment of Japanese Americans began on the day Pearl Harbor was bombed, when Franklin Roosevelt issued a proclamation that declared, in the language of the law, that "all natives, citizens, denizens or subjects of (Japan), being of the age of fourteen years and upward, who shall be in the United States and not actually naturalized, shall be liable to be apprehended, restrained, secured, and removed as alien enemies."[29] Internment, thereby, refers to the parallel but separate process by which mostly Issei men were arrested and detained. The numbers alone are evidence that the internment was a process unto itself. It is estimated that 8,000 Japanese were interned under jurisdiction of the Justice Department,[30] in contrast to the 120,313 persons of Japanese ancestry who were imprisoned by the War Relocation Authority (WRA). In the end, after much consideration and consultation, the National Museum decided to use the terms "concentration camp" and "incarceration" consistently and deliberately in interpreting our experience to the general public.

## First-Person Personal

While the incarceration raises questions of constitutionality, economic loss, and a host of academic, legal, and social concerns—some of which have been addressed while many still need attention—the exhibition America's Concentration Camps sought to provide voice and forum to those whose lives were forever changed by their imprisonment.

In the late 1960s and early 1970s, as the civil rights, antiwar, black power, and women's movements jolted the social conscience of America into facing the country's unsavory side, the many unresolved questions and issues regarding the Japanese American incarceration rose to the surface and burst into view. For decades, schools and textbooks had failed to include, or glossed over, the unprecedented unconstitutional event. And because former inmates rarely spoke about it, we younger Japanese Americans were, in effect, caught in a multilayered conspiracy of silence. We realized that as Asian Americans, we didn't know our own history. We read what little there was, organized pilgrimages to campsites, formed Asian American studies programs on campuses, and cajoled and convinced our parents into finally talking about the camps.

John Kuo Wei Tchen is a historian who, along with Barbara Kirshenblatt-Gimblett, Lonnie Bunch, Claudine Brown, Tomás Ybarra-Fausto, and others, has helped reshape modern museology to be more relevant to diverse—ethnic, regional, and socioeconomic—audiences. Tchen coined the phrase "dialogic exhibit or museum" to refer to a museum actively engaging with its audiences in mutually exploring the history and significance of an exhibit topic or museum mission. He points out that the reflection of one's own history in museum exhibits gives recognition to individuals and groups normally passed over by official versions of history; that the past becomes a touchstone for interpreting and understanding the present and future; and that such acts of self-discovery and recognition shape and reshape individual and collective identities.[31]

In the case of America's concentration camps, where the official account bordered on cover-up, we—as former inmates and Americans as a whole—had long been kept away from the knowledge and understanding of this critical chapter of our personal, community, and national history. To reclaim this neglected past, we enlisted the collaboration of the community of former inmates.

The inmates became the voice of the exhibition. Their experiences and words were transformed into "text panels." Keepsakes they had previously regarded, and often disregarded, as insignificant or having only personal value were now important "artifacts." Instead of relying on official or professional photographs taken by government or news agencies, we used family photos and personal snapshots to emphasize the first-person perspective. In addition to personal memorabilia, survivors contributed official documents and photographs, and even home movies that the public had never seen before.

Considering that cameras were initially regarded as contraband and confiscated at the time of the forced exclusion, it is surprising that a large number of photographs taken by inmates in camp began to surface. Young military draftees and volunteers from camp serving in the U.S. Army returned on leave to visit their parents with cameras in hand. As time passed, restrictions were lifted and inmates mail-ordered cameras from the Montgomery Ward or Sears catalogues—which had become more than simply sources of consumerism but, for the inmates sequestered from American society, vital lifelines to the outside world.

Toyo Miyatake, a professional photographer, sneaked a lens and film holder into Manzanar

Inmates wear serious expressions in one photo but break into laughter in another, showing their determination to lead a normal life in camp. Collection of JANM, gift of Fumi Mochizuki (97.176.1–2).

and built a camera from scrap lumber. An amateur photographer, Toshio Kitagawa, fashioned a darkroom in his barracks by draping an army blanket over a handmade table and digging a hole in the dirt floor in which to stand. After his death, Walter Muramoto's widow found a suitcase filled with photographic negatives and prints of camp life.[32] As they would under ordinary circumstances, these and other inmates took pictures of their children, friends, and life in the making. Besides normalizing life in an abnormal setting, these images provide precious and poignant documentation of life within America's concentration camps.

Even more revealing were 8 mm and 16 mm home movies taken in camp that were discovered while I was curating America's Concentration Camps. In 1989, the veteran filmmaker Robert A. Nakamura and I first came upon home movies taken by Issei as they made America their home. We edited selections from seven collections of 16 mm films taken in the 1920s and 1930s into a three-screen video installation called *Through Our Own Eyes* for the museum's inaugural exhibition on Issei pioneers. It was later contextualized and re-presented for the single screen as *Moving Memories*.[33] Even with this prior experience with home movies, knowing that Japanese Americans were prohibited from having cameras during World War II, Nakamura and I were surprised and excited to discover home movies taken in camp, and we subsequently produced the film *Something Strong Within*, which is discussed in chapter 5.

• • •

While the forced exclusion and unwarranted detention has become a collective community episode, it was and continues to be a private and individual experience. The primacy of the inmates' perspective kept the focus of the exhibition on the particular rather than the general, the personal rather than the anonymous. By reconsidering the traditional authoritative voice of exhibitry and by assuming instead a first-person viewpoint that would reflect the visitor's perspective, we hoped museum goers would identify with the exhibition, personalize history, and thus make the experience meaningful as well as educational.

## 2 / A Strategy of Process and Participation

In preparation for the exhibition, the Japanese American National Museum held many formal and informal meetings with camp survivors. At a community meeting in Seattle, one Nisei woman recalled that a few years earlier, upon watching a documentary about the Holocaust and seeing survivors with numbers that had been tattooed on their arms, she suddenly—after some fifty years—remembered her family's camp identification number. It was like recovering from a spell with amnesia. She said, "All these years I thought I had forgotten it. But it was like it was tattooed on my brain all along."

America's Concentration Camps was designed to introduce the camp experience to a broad audience from the survivors' perspective. By presenting the camps from a first-person viewpoint, the exhibition set the stage for visitors to become active collaborators in reclaiming and telling their own history. The strategy of collaboration was to invite visitors to add their own experiences to the exhibition through a variety of inter-activities. We hoped that by engaging visitors in exploring the memory and meaning of their own histories, they would enter into a personal pilgrimage of reconsidering, reclaiming, and recovering those histories for themselves as well as for others.

Inside the National Museum, the main focus of the exhibition was scale models of each of the camps. Each camp cluster featured layouts of the camp and a stark list of facts and statistics humanized by personal stories and memorabilia. The following text appeared as a wall panel located at the entrance to the exhibition and was also provided to visitors as a handout.

"America's Concentration Camps: Remembering the Japanese American Experience" is a participatory exhibit. We invite all visitors to join us in remembering and better understanding this chapter in American history. Here are ways you can participate:

*Place Your Barracks on the Camp Maps*
If you were in camp, please write your name, family number and camp address in the camp registry located at the entrance to the exhibit. If you are the first person from your barracks to register, you will be given a symbolic barracks model to place directly on the map of your camp in the exhibit.

*Include Your Photo in the Camp Albums*
Former camp inmates and staff are invited to include a Polaroid photograph of themselves in the album located at each camp cluster in the exhibit. Please include your name and dates of incarceration and let us know if you have artifacts or photographs you'd like to loan or donate. If you were in more than one camp, please include your photo in each camp album. Docents will take your picture for $1 per photo.

*Add Your World War II Stories*
Did you live through WWII? Were you incarcerated in one of the detention facilities that is not included in this exhibit? Were you a camp administrator, teacher or guard? Were you or a family member one of the Germans, Italians, or Aleuts who were also incarcerated? Were you one of the many Japanese Americans in Hawai'i, on the East Coast or Midwest who were not incarcerated? Share your experiences and stories. Write them in the book at the conclusion of the exhibition.

*Lost & Found Bulletin Board*
Many people were separated during the war. Many lost contact with friends and neighbors. At the end of the exhibition there is a "bulletin board" for people trying to find lost wartime friends.

*Comment Book*
Please add your comments about the exhibit in the book at the exit.
We'd like to hear from you.

Please ask a docent for more information or assistance.

## Reclaiming the Camps

Despite the introductory nature of the exhibition, we felt it was important to particularize the camps in order to underscore the reality and enormity of the incarceration. Because so many people still did not know or found it hard to believe that the United States had engaged in such an undemocratic procedure, we provided proof of the incarceration camp by camp, rather than offering a generalized representation. Also, because of their personal relationship to the event, camp survivors strongly identified with their particular camp. By presenting each of the eleven camps—the ten War Relocation Center camps and Crystal City—we could underscore the sheer scope of the incident as well as acknowledge the specificity of the camp experience for the survivors.

We decided to include Crystal City because it was the only Justice Department internment camp to contain families. Crystal City was also important in that it contained Japanese Americans from Hawai'i, as well as Japanese Latin American, German American, and some Italian American families.

The eleven camps were presented to contrast the official history—symbolized by a map of the physical site and the cold, hard facts and figures that located that site in historical time and space—with the community memory, which was expressed by the artifacts and stories. We discovered that the modelmaker Robert Hasuike, who had created an elaborate model of Manzanar in the 1980s, had acquired the actual government blueprints for each of the camps. He donated them to the National Museum and they became the basis for the camp maps we exhibited. The irrefutable reality of the incarceration represented by the physical map was made even more acute by the etching of state and city boundaries, other major geographical identifiers such as highways

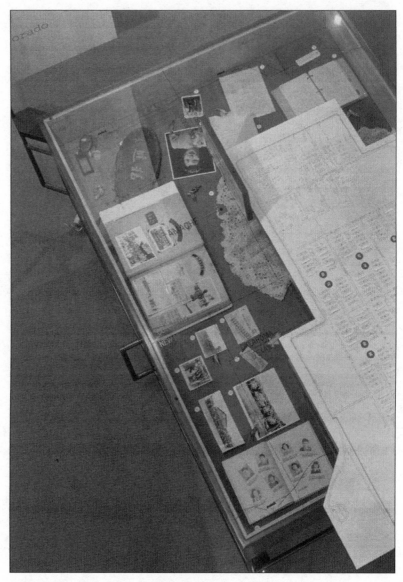

The display case containing artifacts from Amache concentration camp in Colorado is overlaid with the ground plan of the camp. Photograph by Norman H. Sugimoto.

and rivers, and even latitude and longitude onto the glass covering the display cases that held the artifacts and stories.

In order to look into the deeper context of the community memory, the visitor literally had to peer through the cartographical symbols that positioned the camps within the geography of the United States.

### Camp Registries

Camp registries, in the form of simple three-ring binders, were set up for former inmates to sign. There was one for each camp, and survivors were invited to write their own names as well as the names of other family members who resided there, their identification numbers, and their block and barracks numbers. We hoped that the act of remembering—asking their parents, siblings, aunts, and uncles for information or verifying family stories—and the act of signing would be part of the process of reappropriating their experience and would remove the anonymity of victimhood to reinstate names where numbers usually sufficed.

The camp "registration" was originally to take place at a small table at the entrance to the exhibition. Two docents were assigned to assist the visitors. However, at the opening and throughout the first week, the small table became so crowded that two eight-foot tables, staffed by many more volunteer docents, had to be set up downstairs in the museum to accommodate the number of visitors who lined up to sign the camp registries. After the first week, these tables were moved into the exhibition hall, and later Clement Hanami, the museum's in-house designer/fabricator, and Bob Uragami, a retired engineer and dedicated volunteer, designed and built a camp registry/information station as part of the exhibition in order to accommodate the continued numbers of visitors wishing to lay claim to their barracks. This station held cabinets for the camp registries, which—as they grew to two and three binders per camp—totaled twenty-four binders by the end of the exhibition. It housed the hundreds of model barracks and became a center for the distribution of camp-related information as well as impromptu docent-visitor discussions. The registration table thus became a permanent—and popular—installation of the exhibition.

At their peak, the ten WRA camps held from 7,318 (Amache in Colorado) to 18,789 (Tule Lake in California) inmates, with most containing roughly 10,000 people. With such sizable populations, the camps were often larger than many American towns. Within the camps, families were housed in 16' × 20', 20' × 20', or 24' × 20' rooms, euphemistically referred to as "apartments," in row upon row of six-unit wooden, army-style barracks. Single men were usually housed together in separate quarters. Our exhibit designer, Ralph Appelbaum, came up with the idea of having inmates place model barracks on the camp layouts. Motivated to find an economical way to fabricate eleven camp models, he was also mindful of the significance of having the survivors themselves lay claim to their space. Just as we underestimated the appeal of signing the camp registry, neither us of realized just how significant—and emotional—the power of placing the barracks would be.

For the opening day of the exhibition, we selected two of the oldest survivors we knew to ceremoniously place the first barracks on the layouts of the camps where they had lived. Harukichi Nakamura, my eighty-six-year-old father-in-law, placed his barracks on block 36, barracks 2, unit 5, on the Manzanar map.[1]

My father-in-law had been a martial arts instructor. Because so many other instructors were arrested on or soon after December 7, 1941, and were whisked away without being able to take any belongings, he had packed a suitcase in anticipation. For whatever reason, he was not picked up early. On June 1, 1942, however, he was sent with his wife and five-year-old son to Manzanar. His second son was born there in April 1944. After living together in a 20' × 20' barracks unit for almost three years, the family was released, on February 13, 1945, and went to Denver, Colorado, to join Mr. Nakamura's brother before returning to Los Angeles.

Kinuko Ito, my friend Sandy Maeshiro's feisty ninety-six-year-old grandmother, placed her model barracks on the Amache camp map.[2] Mrs. Ito had attended Polytechnic Beauty College in Los Angeles and operated her own salon for thirteen years before being sent first to the

Harukichi Nakamura (center) shows a reporter the model of his barracks on the map of Manzanar as his wife, Kimiko, looks on. Photograph by Robert A. Nakamura.

assembly center at the Santa Anita Race Track and then, on September 24, 1942, as identification number 17910, to Amache in Colorado, along with her husband and two daughters.[3] Her daughters left camp first. She and her husband were released on October 11, 1944, and went to New York before returning to Los Angeles, where Mrs. Ito resumed her career as a beautician. She worked as a beautician—albeit part-time—until she was ninety-seven years old.

Kinuko Ito puts her barracks model on the Amache camp map with the author at her side.
Photograph by Robert A. Nakamura.

Thereafter, visitors who signed the camp registry were given a small wooden model barracks to place on the block where they had lived. The act of placing their barracks on the once barren blueprints symbolized their original act, over fifty years earlier, of peopling some of the most desolate real estate in the United States. The acts of signing the registry, recalling their block and barracks number, and finding and placing the model barracks on the spot where they lived became a private journey of embracing and hence reclaiming a past experience in a new light.

Many did so silently. Others did so out loud, as they spoke of who lived where; the paths to the latrine, laundry room, and school; and other memories in widening circles of remembrance and reclamation. Survivors hoisted up their grandchildren and had them position the model barracks on their behalf, literally and figuratively passing on the legacy of the camps.[4] One man, who was held for a period of time in the camp stockade for political resistance, placed his barracks in the stockade. By actively participating in the fabrication of the camp models, visitors became involved in a process of personal discovery as well as in the collaborative creation of a public display.

Day by day, the camp layouts grew more detailed. Through the eleven-month run of the exhibition, former residents placed a total of 2,276 barracks on the eleven camp maps. Each barracks had six living compartments. Many people were transferred within camps as well as from camp to camp. Therefore one barracks could have been "home" to a multitude of people over its lifetime.

The historian and architect Dolores Hayden later used the camp models and maps as examples of how cultural landscape history can frame the connections between places, memories, and public history. Of the exhibition she wrote, "It shows how the memories of places can be used to stimulate a process of remembrance which begins in a personal way but links private memory to public history and politics."[5] She pointed out that the process of mourning involves memories of places and human connections with those places. In particular, she called attention to the fact that people make connections to places that are critical not only to their well-being but also to their distress. In light of the significance of people's attachment to place, the prevalence of other site-specific events such as camp reunions and pilgrimages are understood as part of the rehabilitative process of recovery rather than as simply nostalgia.

### Camp Albums

At each camp cluster, three-ring notebooks were once again transformed, this time into photo albums that, like the registries, expanded over time. Whether inmate, teacher, guard, or staff—or in some cases their descendants—each former resident was invited to have a docent take their portrait for one dollar and add it to the albums, along with their memories.

By the end of the exhibition, the albums held 3,496 photos. In a silent but significant declaration of ownership and identity, they formed a visual chorus that proclaimed, "I was there." Even more survivors joined the chorus from afar. Inmates who were not able to get to the museum or lived out of town, and even spouses and children representing survivors posthumously, mailed in their photos to be included in the camp albums. This activity was set up at each of the traveling venues, which added hundreds more photographs of survivors to the camp albums. In examining the albums, Dolores Hayden recalled an observation by Hanna Krall about an exhibit of photographs of Polish Jews. Hayden reported that Krall said, "You can't have compassion for the millions, for all those zeroes. The best thing we can do is to give back individual faces to all these people."[6]

Most of the photos in the albums were single portraits of former inmates, but many individuals chose to have their picture taken with other people, indicating the collective and enduring nature of even this private and particular experience. Several people took their pictures with their spouses. Some chose to have their pictures taken with their brothers and sisters, emblematic of the fact that this had been a family experience. Notably absent were their parents, who had passed on.

Many took their photos with their children and grandchildren—most of whom were born after the war and were never in camp. This photo grouping reveals not only that they attended the exhibition as a

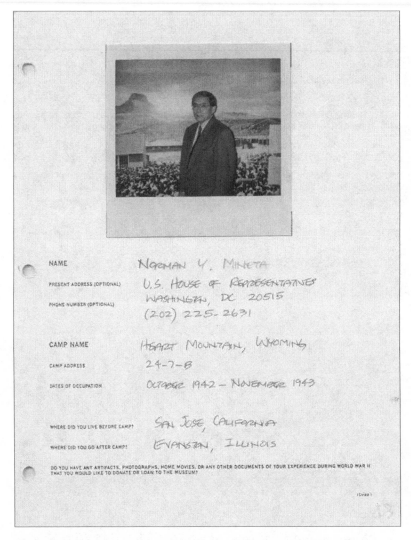

Album page of Norman Y. Mineta. Mineta was an eleven-year-old Cub Scout whose baseball bat was confiscated as a dangerous weapon when he and his family were forced from their home in 1942. Twenty-five years later, he began his public service career, first as a city councilman, then as mayor of San Jose, California, and later as a U.S. congressman and secretary of transportation. Collection of JANM.

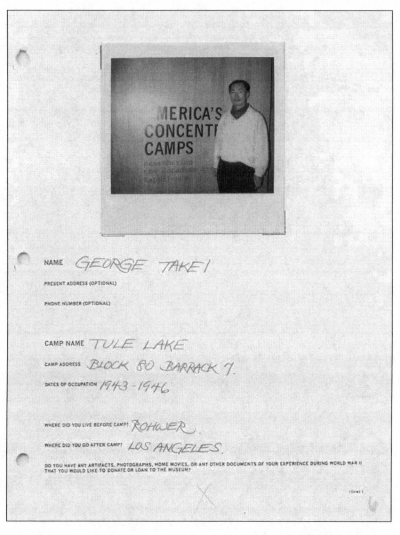

NAME *GEORGE TAKEI*

PRESENT ADDRESS (OPTIONAL)

PHONE NUMBER (OPTIONAL)

CAMP NAME *TULE LAKE*

CAMP ADDRESS *BLOCK 80 BARRACK 7.*

DATES OF OCCUPATION *1943 - 1946*

WHERE DID YOU LIVE BEFORE CAMP? *ROHWER.*

WHERE DID YOU GO AFTER CAMP? *LOS ANGELES.*

DO YOU HAVE ANY ARTIFACTS, PHOTOGRAPHS, HOME MOVIES, OR ANY OTHER DOCUMENTS OF YOUR EXPERIENCE DURING WORLD WAR II THAT YOU WOULD LIKE TO DONATE OR LOAN TO THE MUSEUM?

Veteran actor George Takei, shown on his album page, was five years old when he and his family were taken from their home in Los Angeles, California. Collection of JANM.

family but also that the former inmates wished to include their extended families as part of their personal experience. Once again, like having a grandchild place a barracks on the camp model, this inclusive act, captured in a photo, is a tangible way in which the legacy of the camp experience is passed on to ensuing generations.

A few photos represented the original inmate only in absentia or as representation and memory. In the cases where the resident had passed on, a descendant—by blood or even friendship—was invited to include his or her own picture in memory of the deceased. One man came to the exhibition prepared; he had his picture taken holding up a photo of his father.

On the back of each album page we posed questions that elicited a range of memories. "What is your fondest memory of camp? Your worst? What is the one thing you would like to tell your children, fellow Americans, or the world about your camp experience?" The memories that were shared reflected both collective themes and a wonderfully wide variety of specific experiences, such as "softening pages of Montgomery Ward catalogue to use as toilet paper." The most common fond memory was of the lasting friendships and relationships that were formed in camp: "sharing fears, ideas, and hopes." Many people mentioned they met their spouses in camp. "Our romance started in camp and it was unforgivable because we were spied upon by the soldiers in the lookout tower and they used their search light, . . . the intense light focusing directly on our faces. Thank God that it was just like a bad dream, but we will never, never forgive them." Effectively separated from the outside world by ethnicity and barbed wire, yet psychologically and physically bound together against a common enemy, or in this case—*as* the common enemy—the survivors experienced an intensity of bonding, like that of soldiers in combat, which was reinforced by internal and external forces.

Memories of the worst experiences were numerous and varied. They included: "Having to leave my seriously ill father in the hospital in Los Angeles. My father died one month after we were in camp and my mother and his three daughters could not be with him at the end." "Seeing so many boys go off to war and dying." "I was held back by the

FBI at the gate when I tried to board a bus to attend a college in Michigan. I was not released until early '45 to attend U.C. Berkeley as the first group to test the reaction at the U.C. campus during WWII." "Returning to California and having to adjust to the 'outside' life when prejudice was still so strong." "Seeing my parents lose everything they worked so hard to earn."

Since most of the remaining survivors are Nisei who had been children, teenagers, or young adults in camp, a common theme they expressed was admiration for the suffering and strength of their Issei parents. One person wrote, "My parents taught us to try not to be bitter but to live each day as it comes in thankfulness." A man shared how his family was split up: "I had three brothers in the U.S. Army while we were in camp. My father could take it no more and we became a no-no family. We (my mother and three sisters) were sent to Tule Lake, which was like a prison. My father and two brothers were sent to other camps. I never saw my father again."[7] Another wrote, "My experiences in camp cannot be compared with those of my parents. They taught me a great deal about 'shinbo' [endurance, perseverance] and making the best of circumstances, no matter how tough they may be."

Many responses were more than just recollections. One survivor wrote, "My worst memory of camp was the realization (to my young eyes) that my freedom was curtailed and that the guns held by the guards were pointed at me. Further, it is difficult to maintain strong self-esteem when your worth as a human being is so strongly questioned."

By far, the most common remark—which took on the tone of plea, supplication, admonishment, and exhortation—was that it never happen again. "No other peoples should be so incarcerated for just being." "Tell other Americans: Never let this happen again to *anyone* in the U.S." "I would lay down my life to make sure something like this would *not* happen again." "That looking back on my primitive emotions following the Oklahoma City bombing of May 1995, and realizing that I was falling victim to the very prejudices that put us in the camps. It certainly can happen again."

Rachel Naomi Remen, a physician and author, writes, "Sitting around the table telling stories is not just a way of passing time. It is the way wisdom gets passed along." The following memories taken from the camp albums disclose the many true stories that, in Remen's words, have "no beginning and ending. They are a front-row seat to the real experience. Even though they may have happened in a different time or place they have a familiar feel. In some way they are about us, too."[8]

> We went into a market for sodas and when we came out we met a posse with drawn guns who herded us back over the bridge and stated they did not want Japs in their town and stay on the other side of the bridge.

> Used to sneak away from camp to go fishing. A friend of mine ran a bookie operation from within the camp. During one of the riots a man standing next to me was shot and killed.

> When the Japanese were notified of being sent to the camps, a customer of my Dad's who was an FBI agent sent his wife to tell my dad he was willing to hide my family. He didn't believe the Japanese should have been relocated to camps. My father refused his offer saying that the government was sending us and we had to go.

> I remember going out to McGhee and pondering which restroom— "colored" or "white"—to use. Finally chose "colored" but was stopped by a white lady and told I was "white."

## Comment Books

At the end of the exhibition space were comment books, a common addendum to most museum exhibits as a means to solicit feedback. However, we invited visitors not only to remark on the exhibition but also to share their own experiences, thoughts, and feelings about the incarceration and World War II. One comment book was simply labeled "Comments." The other was labeled "This Too Is Our Story." Like the other opportunities to add to the exhibition and interact with it, the results overwhelmed our expectations.

Over fifteen hundred visitors wrote comments. Some remarks were about the exhibition itself. Although most were complimentary, some people expressed their desire for more information. For example, one person wrote, "Though I found the exhibit informative, I felt it barely touched the goal we are trying to reach. My heart aches for more." A number of visitors added such compelling stories, questions, and responses that the comment books, like the camp albums, became an integral part of the exhibition, read by visitors as carefully as the formal text panels and other elements. Many respondents added their own memories of camp: "Wish I was older during camp days so I could really remember and understand all that happened in those days. I was a teenager so I did not realize how serious the situation was."

Some comments were from third-, fourth-, and fifth-generation Japanese Americans who expressed their personal connection to an event they had never directly experienced: "Because I am a yonsei (fourth-generation Japanese American) I was never in the camps, but through my grandparents' silence and shame it was passed down to me. It hasn't been until recently that I realized it is my duty now to ask questions, to write it down, and make sure we all remember."

Some offspring of survivors addressed their comments to their parents: "Mom, Dad & Nanny—I never really understood camp life. . . . Now that I am a mother, I can't fathom my children enduring this. Nanny, this must have been so painful. . . . It all hit me on really how much you must have went through."

Visitors even responded to others' comments. To the inquiry "I have a question, did any mixed, Japanese-white people get put in the camps?" two people answered, "Yes, a half Japanese is Japanese as well as a half Afro-American is black in this country." "Tiffany—The answer to your question is yes. My best friend in the third grade class in Poston, Arizona, Camp 1 was mixed or 'happa.'"

Some wrote their comments in Japanese. And people of other ethnicities were obviously moved by the exhibition, a point that was poignantly illustrated by one person who taped an image of the Virgin de Guadalupe to a page of a comment book. The following are examples that attest that the camps not only affected former inmates or just members of the Japanese American community but touched all conscientious people attempting to live decently and do well by others:

I am a Chicano, born and raised in L.A. This display touches my soul. . . . When will this nation learn from its mistakes?

As an American and as a Jew we must remember what happened here and never forget.

In 1967 I was a good student but was flunked by my history teacher, Mr. Blunt, for daring to write a critical report on the internment. I am glad we are no longer required to be silent on the subject.

As an African American I am touched by what I have seen here and in my own way, I share the pain that those remembered here must feel. My hope is that this museum live on for all generations of Americans yet to be born to see so that they might know the danger of racism that goes unchallenged.

## California Proposition 187

The exhibition opened one week after California voters passed the highly controversial Proposition 187, which denied public services to people who reside illegally in California. Immigration and immigrants' rights proved to be as contentious an issue in the 1990s as it was in the early 1900s, when the California legislature passed the Alien Land Law (1913), which made it illegal for aliens ineligible for citizenship to own or lease land.[9] While the immigrant groups under attack were never named, the fact that the Alien Land Law targeted Asian immigrants was as apparent as the fact that Proposition 187 targeted Latinos. The exhibition visitors themselves brought up the parallel between these issues so often, in the comment books and in conversation, that this subject became an unexpected but undeniable part of the exhibition. There were such comments as:

> I am a Mexican—second generation. Proposition 187 was recently passed by a majority vote. It seems that America is still struggling with the issue of exclusion, exclusion by color/ethnicity. It is a shame that people of color have to prove themselves in this land of immigrants, generation after generation.

> I cannot help but compare our treatment of the Japanese then, Indians and African American before, to the plight of Hispanics today. Have we not learned anything? Are we not all created equal?

With the recent passage of Proposition 187, we are seeing the same racism, xenophobia, hysteria and general lack of political leadership similar to what happened to Japanese Americans more than fifty years ago. . . . With almost half of the Asian American voters who voted this year supporting this racist proposition, we still have much work to do.

As a Mexican American I can relate to the racist comments in the print media. Actually, with the recent anti-immigrant sentiment in California, this exhibition reminds all of us how precious our so-called democracy really is.

My dad's side of the family went through the Holocaust. My mom's side is suffering greatly from 187. I *can* begin to imagine what it was like for the Japanese.

## Lost and Found

From the museum's beginning, the staff periodically received calls from people in search of friends and relatives with whom they had lost touch through the years of dislocation and resettlement. In another effort to make the exhibition responsive to our constituency and engage their participation and involvement, we included a "Lost and Found" bulletin board as part of it. Through the course of the exhibition, twenty-nine notes were posted on the board, their brevity and simplicity undoubtedly belying the ardor of their writers. Some of these notes said:

> To Lewis Kazumi and my other classmates who disappeared so abruptly one day in 1942 from 24th School in Los Angeles: I hope all is well with you. . . . I wonder where you are now, wish you the best and hope we can meet somewhere someday.

> Anyone knowing my grandfather, Shuzo Takeuchi, Poston from Stanton, CA and released to Utah area please contact Jan at [phone number]. [On this note someone wrote, "There is a Takeuchi family in Cincinnati. . . . Perhaps they are familiar with Shuzo Takeuchi."]

> Anyone knowing the phone number of any of the Hagio Family of San Juan Capistrano please call Ken [phone number]. Thank you, An old school chum.

I spent kindergarten and 1st grade in Topaz. Would like to hear about classmates. Jim Jennings, Santa Maria, [phone number].

One note, from "Rebecca's daughter Joanne," remarkably ended a fifty-two-year search to help reconstruct the writer's past. Joanne was six years old when her mother died during the war. The strongest link Joanne had to her mother was the memory of a Japanese American woman she knew only as Toshi, who had helped care for and soon befriended her sick mother before the war. Without any living grand-mothers or involved relatives, Joanne remembered Toshi as a key figure. Joanne recalled hearing that Toshi had to leave suddenly. She learned that her mother had visited Toshi while she was detained at the Santa Anita assembly center. Because of the makeshift, crowded conditions of communal life, one of the most coveted possessions for a young mother with diapers to wash was a washboard and tub, which Rebecca had pro-vided. Joanne knew that her mother and Toshi had corresponded until Rebecca's death in 1943.

As Joanne grew up, got married, and became a mother and grand-mother herself, she thought more of the mother she barely knew yet deeply missed. She told me that although she could not regain her mother, perhaps she could find Toshi. And so—without even knowing her last name—Joanne began her search for Toshi. She placed an ad in the classified section of a Japanese-language paper. She asked Japanese Americans she happened to meet. She searched through high school yearbooks in the location and time period in which she thought Toshi might have graduated.

Joanne said she had been searching for years and was just about to abandon her effort when her sister Judy, who happened to come to the museum during her lunch hour, called to tell her that not only was there an exhibition on the Japanese American incarceration but there was a bulletin board in it that seemed meant for her. Bolstered by the knowledge that she was not alone in her search to find lost friends, Joanne came to the exhibition and posted a note that stated, "Looking for 'Toshi' who knew my mother Rebecca Grossman and helped her in the house around 1940 on Blackburn Ave. L.A. Please call [phone number]. Rebecca's daughter Joanne."

At the museum, Joanne made friends with Lily Oba, the coordinator of volunteers, and together they combed through the thousands of photos in the camp albums for women named Toshi. One friend, Take Miyatake, suggested to the editor of the *Rafu Shimpo,* one of the oldest Japanese American vernacular presses in the country, that the paper run a story on Joanne's search. The resulting article began, "Daughters who lost their mother while still very young are forever searching for the past. . . . And Joanne Gertzman, 59, is no exception."[10]

The very day the article appeared, two people responded with the

## IN SEARCH OF ...

### Woman Seeks Late Mother's Former Helper

Daughters who lost their mother while still very young are forever searching for the past. The journey of looking for continuity in family history becomes more important as the daughters become mothers, and grandmothers, in their turn. And Joanne Gertzman, 59, is no exception.

Gertzman's mother, Rebecca Grossman, died from cancer in 1943 when Joanne was 7 years old. There are few memories left when the loss came at such an early age. But one thing Gertzman remembers quite well was her mother's warm friendship with a woman named Toshi, who was mother's helper.

Gertzman remembers Toshi coming to their house at 8420 Blackburn in Los Angeles when she was just 4 years old. She also remembers Toshi leaving soon after for one of the camps set up by the U.S. for people of Japanese descent.

Her mother and Toshi corresponded during those internment years, but the letter have long since been lost. There was one more contact with Toshi, when she visited Joanne and her sisters in the 1950s on her way to Chicago. That was the last contact between Toshi and the Grossman family.

"In my head, I've been searching for so long," said Gertzman, who has placed ads and investigated camp records at the Japanese American National Museum. She does not recall Toshi's family name, nor where she might live today. All of her mother's siblings have since passed away.

Gertzman currently resides in Los Angeles, and has children of her own, as well as grandchildren.

Anyone with information that may help Gertzman is encouraged to call (213) 651-2327, or write to 416 N. Orlando Ave., Los Angeles, CA 90048.

Toshi, here holding the baby, is seen here with the Grossman fam in this photo, dated at approximately 1940-41. Joanne (Grossm Gertzman, the older girl in front, is now 59, and wants to find T to learn more about her late mother, Rebecca, also pictured. Gertzm was 7 years old when her mother died. The man in the photo co possibly be Toshi's husband, and the baby, her child.

Article from the *Rafu Shimpo* telling of Joanne Gertzman's search for Toshi Hieshima. Collection of JANM, courtesy of the *Rafu Shimpo.*

name and phone number of a Toshi in Chicago who seemed to fit the description. Then Toshi herself called. After many disappointments, Joanne was doubtful but hopeful. She asked the woman question after question to which only "her" Toshi would have known the answers. Her long search had finally paid off.

The two women arranged a reunion at the National Museum when Toshi visited Los Angeles the following year. Joanne and Toshi have kept in close touch, and every time they speak, Joanne discovers more details to fill in the gaps in her history. Toshi told Joanne that when her mother visited her in Santa Anita, since she was not allowed to enter and Toshi was not allowed to go out, they held each other's forefingers through the chain link fence. She said that she took the valued washboard and tub to Jerome, then to Rohwer, both in Arkansas, and has it still. In my discussions with Joanne about her story, I told her that although I grew up with a loving stepmother, I too had lost a mother at a young age. Joanne shared that information with Toshi and, to our surprise and delight, we learned that Toshi and her family had known my mother and her family before the war. To pay special tribute to her mother and Toshi, Joanne and her siblings Richard, Judy, and Marilyn made a donation to the National Museum. Joanne said she wanted their names, Rebecca Grossman and Toshi Hieshima—one American Jew and one Japanese American—"etched together in friendship forever."[11]

• • •

We hoped these low-key, low-tech activities in the exhibition would be culturally compatible opportunities for a group that has historically been silenced and for whom quiet perseverance has been both a virtue and a tool of survival.

The numbers of visitors who participated signified that these were indeed simple yet salient acts. Scholars, too, found value in them. The historian Lon Yuki Kurashige, wrote, "Interactive displays, which ask former internees to contribute to the record, breathe life into this reconstruction of their past."[12] Jamie Purinton, a landscape architect, wrote, "In the model and albums, the narratives of many individuals, laid over official government blueprints of the campsite plans, represent a repossession of the power to tell one's own story."[13] The historian David Yoo contextualized the exhibition as playing a role in the "shifting community politics of remembrance." He wrote,

> In very tangible ways, then, the exhibit not only told the story of internment, but served as a touchstone for Japanese Americans. The maps and models of the barracks and the albums allowed people to add their own pieces to the larger story. The random nature of the comments . . . bore witness to the reality that memories resist any single version or interpretation. . . . The photos and binders physically and psychologically altered the shape of the exhibit. For survivors, the interchange encouraged acts of self-discovery (and self-recovery) that not only reevaluated the past, but also enabled individuals and communities to significantly transform their perspectives of the present and the future.[14]

In these quiet ways, the audience became active participant-collaborators who dismantled conventions of authority and control and altered the process of exhibitry as well as its outcome.

A few years before the exhibition, the museum received two suitcases filled with negatives and photographs of camp. The photos had been taken by Walter Muramoto, an amateur photographer who had long been deceased, and they were donated by his widow, who, having married him after the war, knew nothing about these extraordinary images. I found a particularly poignant portrait of a young girl resolutely playing a violin against the backdrop of barracks. Without words, it captured the irony of trying to carry on a normal life in abnormal conditions.

We used the photograph in the exhibition as well as in the special issue of the museum's quarterly featuring the exhibition.[1] Soon after the show opened, I received a call from Yuki Tamura Yamamoto. She said that upon receiving the quarterly in the mail, she kept looking at the photo, thinking that the girl somehow looked familiar. She showed it to her husband, who asked, "Isn't that you?" When she brought her family to see the exhibition, her grandson pointed to her photo and proudly exclaimed, "Oh, Grandma, you're part of history!"[2]

Yuki Tamura practicing her violin in Rohwer. Collection of JANM, gift of the Walter Muramoto Family (97.293.10).

## Taking Back the Barracks

The main focus of the exhibition, which was mounted in two areas, was on the camps themselves. Outside, in a parking lot across the street from the National Museum, the physicality of the camps asserted itself in the urban landscape of downtown Los Angeles with a full-sized camp barracks, some 120 feet long. The barracks, half of which was original and half of which was reconstructed to show the building's original size, was flanked on one side by a 25-foot-high guard tower and on the other side by a massive 10' × 30' billboard that bore the words, "America's Concentration Camps: Remembering the Japanese American Experience, November 11, 1994–October 15, 1995." The three structures were surrounded by a chain-link fence.

The barracks owed its presence to a collective act of reconstructing history that started with Harumi "Bacon" Sakatani, a former Heart Mountain inmate. Since joining the museum staff in 1989, I had heard about Bacon and his seemingly farfetched idea of bringing an actual barracks to Los Angeles. He was steadfast to the point of obsession and negotiated with the museum for years until at last, on the occasion of the exhibition, he prevailed. His victory was won for all of us as the barracks became a bold and defiant symbol of a people reclaiming their past.

After the war, the original 20' × 120' barracks were sold, reportedly for a dollar each, to local ranchers and homesteaders who sawed them up into smaller units and used them for everything from warehouses to residences. After over fifty years, most of the original barracks had disintegrated. But Sakatani and the National Museum found two barracks at Heart Mountain in Wyoming, which were donated to the museum, one by the Tak Ogawa family, the other by Marion and Rod Morrison. Each building was roughly 20' × 60', half the size of an original barracks. The Ogawa barracks, whose interior was well preserved, would be put into storage for future presentation in our new building. The Morrison barracks, whose exterior had not been altered, would be rebuilt, along with new construction to show its original size, to become the exhibition's most dramatic symbol.

A chain-link fence surrounded the outdoor portion of the exhibition. It consisted of a re-constructed guard tower; a barracks, half of which was original; and a billboard announc-ing the exhibition. Photograph by Norman H. Sugimoto.

In September 1994, volunteers answered a request from Nancy Ara-ki, the National Museum's director of community affairs, to go to Heart Mountain to bring back the barracks. With the conviction of a divine mission, friends and strangers went to symbolically and literally take back one of the camp's original barracks. It was an enormous undertak-ing, both physically and emotionally. After Sakatani negotiated with the museum, the museum negotiated with city hall for permits to erect such a structure on city property. Thirty-two volunteers, many of whom, like my uncle George Iseri, had been incarcerated at Heart Mountain, con-tended with uncertain weather conditions, missed flights, lost luggage, and ambivalent memories to get to the obscure spot between Cody and Powell, Wyoming, where the barracks were located. Under the direc-tion of Jim McElwain, a preservation architect, and David Honda, a contractor, the volunteers carefully dismantled the barracks board by board, pulling out deep-seated emotions with every nail. Returning to Los Angeles, they and many others painstakingly put the building to-

The author's uncle, George Iseri (foreground), a former inmate at Heart Mountain, was among the volunteers who, in 1994, dismantled a camp barracks there for reassembly at the Japanese American National Museum. Courtesy of George Iseri.

gether again, making it the largest—and most arresting—artifact in the exhibition.[3]

One volunteer, Sharon Yamato Danley, was so moved by the experience that she would write and publish a booklet recounting the ordeal.[4] In an interview in the *Los Angeles Times*, she said she saw a man who could have been her father, fighting back tears as he worked. "Although no one could deny that preserving these barracks fostered joyful camaraderie and a tremendous sense of accomplishment, this project meant so much more to him. The barracks were not just artifacts to be put on display at a museum. They were a tangible part of this life, a part that he would rather have forgotten but knew he could not."[5]

"This is my boyhood home," Sakatani said after the barracks had been resurrected in Los Angeles. "Taking back the barracks is taking our whole experience back to California for our children to see."[6] Stan Honda, who would be known to the world for his chilling photographs of survivors of the attacks on the World Trade Center on September 11, 2001, volunteered, photographed, and wrote about recovering the barracks. He said, "The experience reminded me that my father, my mother, my aunts and uncles and cousins were part of history, part of American history, part of something that should not be forgotten."[7]

## Docents as Living Artifacts

The importance of the docents in this type of participatory exhibition was immense. In staffing the camp registry, handing out 2,276 model barracks, and taking 3,496 Polaroid pictures, they were critical in the success of these activities. Because of the first-person emphasis of the exhibition, docents who were former inmates also became "living artifacts" in the exhibit hall and an essential part of the interpretive strategy of process and participation. Docents who were not former inmates were also encouraged to personalize history by sharing their own stories from their particular vantage point. Those who lived through World War II were urged to recount their own memories of that time and how the war affected them. Younger ones were asked to think about and convey how this past was relevant to their present.[8]

The museum is fortunate to have a large cadre of volunteers. Hard working and dedicated, good spirited and warm hearted, they are a never-ending source of inspiration. They have become role models for the museum staff and, since there are so many who volunteer as couples, they are particularly inspiring for my husband and work partner, Bob, and me. Margaret and Dave, Lois and Elman, Lili and Tadd, Bob and Rumi, and so many others set a new standard of partnership. In addition to the thirty-two hours of formal training the docents received, I conducted formal and informal discussions with docents and other museum volunteers throughout the development of the exhibition. Because most of them were former inmates, they were as interested in learning how the exhibition was progressing as I was in hearing their stories, seeing their photographs and artifacts, and learning from their experiences.

To foster the engagement between docent and visitor at the exhibition, docents wore name badges featuring photos of themselves during the war years and emblazoned with the invitation, "Ask me about America's Concentration Camps." Below each docent's photo was the name of the camp where he or she lived, which brought out the particularity of the experience. Picturing the docents as they were in wartime underscored the continuity between the past and the present. Besides, it was a kick to see them as kids, teens, and young adults. Some of the docents continue to use these name badges even though the exhibition has long been over.

One of the late Lois Padilla's most memorable experiences as a docent was the time she oriented a woman to the camp albums containing the on-the-spot Polaroid photos taken of visitors who had lived in particular camps. This visitor, like so many others, not only added her own image but perused the pages of the album to see who else from her camp had become part of the exhibition. Doing so, the woman let out a yelp and, with the momentarily recaptured giddiness of a teenager, excitedly told Lois, "I found my first boyfriend!" However, immediately transported back to the future, she added, "But he got so old!"

As an active docent throughout the run of the exhibition, Ike Hatchimonji witnessed—and felt—a myriad of emotions. He observed many

Ask Me... about **AMERICA'S CONCENTRATION CAMPS**

Amache

Lois Padilla

JAPANESE AMERICAN NATIONAL MUSEUM

Lois Padilla's docent badge. JANM.

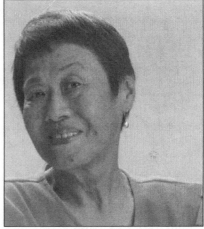

Lois Padilla in 1995. JANM. Photograph by Norman H. Sugimoto.

tearful reunions of former inmates who had not seen each other since camp. He became the subject of term papers and was quoted in news articles. He was also told, "You Japs bombed Pearl Harbor so you deserved what you got!" As Ike pointed out, such a statement reveals that some still cannot or choose not to make the distinction between Americans of Japanese ancestry and Japanese soldiers.

Ike Hatchimonji in 1995. JANM. Photograph by Norman H. Sugimoto.

Ask Me...
about
**AMERICA'S
CONCENTRATION
CAMPS**

Heart Mountain

Ike Hatchimonji

JAPANESE AMERICAN
NATIONAL MUSEUM

Ike Hatchimonji's docent badge. JANM.

Another docent, Masako Koga Murakami, said that for her, one story summed up the impact of the exhibition. She brought a reluctant friend who had never talked about camp and was disinclined to see the exhibition. Her family, like Masako's, had been uprooted and separated more than once during the course of the war. By the close of the exhibition, this friend had returned five times, on each occasion bringing

Tule Lake

Masako Koga

JAPANESE AMERICAN
NATIONAL MUSEUM

Masako Koga Murakami's docent badge. JANM.

Masako Koga Murakami in 1995. JANM. Photograph by Norman H. Sugimoto.

someone else. She brought her sister, who had gone to Japan right after the war, returned as an adult, and never talked about their incarceration or their separation until visiting the exhibition. She brought her boss, and another time she brought her children. The exhibition acted as a bridge between herself and at least five significant others, and perhaps even between her present and her past.

Margaret Masuoka in 1995. JANM. Photograph by Norman H. Sugimoto.

Ask Me...
about
**AMERICA'S CONCENTRATION CAMPS**

Poston

Margaret Masuoka

JAPANESE AMERICAN
NATIONAL MUSEUM

Margaret Masuoka's docent badge. JANM.

David and Margaret Masuoka were known for their abiding love story. Having met and fallen in love before the war, they were together in the Santa Anita assembly center but were sent to separate camps—he to Gila River and she to Poston. Both of them refused to be married in a concentration camp and so they waited and they wrote to one another. As part of what little she could take to Poston, Margaret had selected a

Ask Me...
about
**AMERICA'S CONCENTRATION CAMPS**

Gila

David Masuoka

JAPANESE AMERICAN
NATIONAL MUSEUM

David Masuoka's docent badge. JANM.

David Masuoka in 1995. JANM. Photograph by Norman H. Sugimoto.

wooden-handled purse, a monogrammed jewelry box, and a wooden pin carved into an "M"—all crafted by Dave in Santa Anita and displayed in the exhibition. The docents liked to point out these objects and tell the story of the Masuokas as proof that, as rotten and unjust as camp had been, love and the human spirit were stronger.

## Remembering Pearl Harbor

The exhibition opened and enjoyed a successful run without any expressed opposition. We were relieved that it received no public criticism, although we had been prepared to deal with it. We had paved the way by meeting with people and organizations that might have misunderstood our intent to educate a broad public. However, the people we met with were not the ones who might raise problems. From the beginning we were cognizant of the general racism and bigotry that exists in this country as well as the bitter feelings that still festered among veterans and their families who suffered greatly during World War II.

We conducted staff and volunteer training on how to handle hostilities, from rude remarks to bomb threats. I learned from Lois Padilla's quick wit during a role-playing session on how to deal with hostile remarks. When asked how she would reply to the allegation, "Well, what did you expect after you bombed Pearl Harbor?!" she replied without hesitation, "Yes, wasn't that terrible! We were so scared. I was only ten and we were coming home from church and . . ."

### Before Pearl Harbor

At the turn of the twentieth century, while Europeans immigrated to the East Coast, Japanese came to Hawai'i and the West Coast. However, Japanese and other Asian immigrants were prohibited from becoming naturalized U.S. citizens until as late as 1952. This meant that during World War II, Japanese immigrants, who otherwise might have wished to become citizens, remained outside the protection of the U.S. Constitution. This denial of citizenship provided the legal basis of decades of anti-Asian sentiment that in turn paved the way for the mass incarceration.

In comparison to the thirty million immigrants from Europe who came to the United States between the 1860s and 1930, in 1930 there were fewer than 140,000 immigrants from Japan.[9] Discrimination against the Japanese was institutionalized, despite the fact that they comprised only one-tenth of 1 percent of the U.S. population. Alien Land Laws were passed that prohibited aliens who were ineligible for citizenship from owning land. Antimiscegenation laws prohibited interracial marriage, and women who married aliens ineligible for citizenship would lose their own citizenship. Labor unions barred Japanese and other Asians from becoming members. The Asiatic Exclusion League, a coalition of 231 organizations at its height, worked to curb further immigration of Japanese to the United States. And in 1924 Congress passed the Immigration Exclusion Act, which denied all further immigration from Japan.

Despite the manifest attempts to prevent them from doing so, Japanese made America their home. In the exhibition, this contradictory environment, teeming with possibility and high hopes as well as hostility and discrimination, was represented in a panel entitled "Before the War." Fifty years of anti-Asian sentiment had set the stage for the eventual mass removal and incarceration of Japanese Americans. After Pearl Harbor was attacked, the government's response to the public outcry for retaliation and revenge lay with these Americans who had the face of the enemy.

Unknown to the public at the time, government agencies covertly kept tabs on leaders in the Japanese American communities throughout the West Coast and Hawai'i during the decade before World War II. Despite the Munson Report of November 1941, which concluded that Japanese Americans posed no threat to national security and would be loyal to the United States in the event of war, over seven hundred Japanese American leaders—including two of my grandfathers—were arrested by the FBI within twenty-four hours of the bombing of Pearl Harbor.

Most of these people were transferred to internment camps run by the Justice Department. On February 19, 1942, President Franklin D. Roosevelt signed Executive Order 9066. While not specifically naming Japanese Americans, the order enabled the circumvention of constitutional safeguards and provided the authority for the mass exclusion and incarceration of Japanese nationals, who were not allowed to become naturalized citizens, as well as their children who were American-born citizens.

The author's grandfather Momota Okura, shown in the 1930s, was a proud and distinguished gentleman. Courtesy of Frances Etsuko Okura.

BASIC PERSONNEL RECORD
(Alien Enemy or Prisoner of War)

ISN-24-4-J-99-CI
(Internment serial number)

OKURA, Momota
(Name of internee)

Male
(Sex)

ISN-24-4-J-99-CI

Fort Missoula, Montana.
(Date and place where processed (Army enclosure, naval station, or other place))

01237

F.P.C. (22) 0 31 W IMM 13
          0 28 W 0 I M

Reference *

Height  5  ft.  8  in.

Weight  161

Eyes  Brown

Skin  Yellow

Hair  Black-grey

Age  59

Distinguishing marks or characteristics:

Mole on right cheek.

INVENTORY OF PERSONAL EFFECTS TAKEN FROM INTERNEE

1.  1-pocket knife
2.
3.
4.
5.
6.
7.
8.
9.
10.

The above is correct:

Momota Okura
(Signature of internee)

**Right Hand**

| 1. Thumb | 2. Index finger | 3. Middle finger | 4. Ring finger | 5. Little finger |
|---|---|---|---|---|

**Left Hand**

| 6. Thumb | 7. Index finger | 8. Middle finger | 9. Ring finger | 10. Little finger |
|---|---|---|---|---|

W. D., P. M. G. Form No. 2
December 9, 1941

Note amputations in proper space

* Do not fill in.

Momota Okura was picked up by the FBI after midnight on December 7, 1941, and taken to the immigration station at Terminal Island. He was sent to four different internment camps before being reunited with his family in Jerome, two years later. This identification card, titled "Basic Personnel Record," designated him as an "Alien Enemy or Prisoner of War." National Archives (NRC1997.44.11).

## Responses to Direct Mail Appeal

The museum used the topic of the camps and the occasion of the exhibition as the focus of a direct-mail fundraising appeal. The appeal succeeded in bringing in not only donations and memberships, but a range of opinions as well. Many were supportive and came from a variety of people: "As a survivor of the Holocaust who lost all of his family I greatly sympathize with you." "I am so glad that you have chosen to use the word concentration camp instead of internment camp or relocation center." "I wish I could give more. The tragic and sad experience of Japanese Americans in this country in WWII must be a reminder that no such tragedy should ever happen again."

Fred Brooks wrote, "As you can see, I made my first protest many years ago," referring to an enclosed photocopy of a newspaper dated February 25, 1947, in which his letter-to-the-editor began, "Your recent editorial defending the removal and confinement of Japanese and American citizens of Japanese origin demonstrates the results of muddled thinking and a disregard for the facts." The letter continued, "Liberty is either enjoyed by everyone or by no one. If any group of citizens can be deprived of their liberties without trial none of us is safe from similar treatment." Brooks ended his letter by noting, "I spent four years overseas during the war fighting for freedom—not concentration camps labeled, 'Made in America.'"[10]

Some recipients were offended at receiving the direct mail appeal and let us know: "F**k you, you stupid Japs! Go to hell, all of you. You can't call yourselves American, you Nips. We will never let you take over this country!" "Take your cars back home and stop your buying of America—I just wish people who come to America would love her and not try to do her in." "Go f**k yourselves you gooks."

Some were reasonable though misguided: "My request is please do not let any tax dollars go toward this expense. We cannot afford such a luxury. Japan made a mistake in attacking America. America made a mistake in the camps."

Others remarks can be understood, but not ignored, as scars of personal loss experienced during the war. One person wrote, "They went to camp—I went to war. These Jap/Ams didn't die or were tortured as were my friends in [the] Pacific by the Japs. Forget it!" Another observed, "Every U.S. serviceman suffered loss of individual freedom. And many were also killed or died from internment in Japanese 'death camps.' . . . Every Japanese-American internee should have been proud to make that sacrifice to remove any suspicion of sabotage that obviously existed."

The notion of relative deprivation—in which individuals or groups subjectively perceive themselves as disadvantaged in relationship to others with similar attributes—surfaced in comments many times, in many ways. One person said, "I will not give one cent for your cause. What about our boys on the Bataan March? There is no comparison in the way the Japs treated our boys and the concentration camps." Another wrote, "The camps here were a disgraceful chapter of US history but this is a very offensive equaling term to the ones with gas ovens, torture and tattoos. Anne Frank didn't have dances and a scout troop."

The impulse to compare suffering emerged not only in relationship to the atrocities committed by the Japanese and the horrors of the Holocaust but with regard to Americans Indians and African Americans as well. One person wrote, "Treatment of Native Americans and Blacks was far worse. At least your lives were safe!" Another typed a full-page letter to say, "I want to mention just a few things which make the cruel mistreatment of the Japanese citizens during the second World War seem mild." First she said that our country was established "by murdering for every mile acquired. The persecution of the Indians still goes on today." Second, she stated that "chattel slavery was the system of the United States and economic slavery still exists today." Her third point was that "what our government considered concentration camps were not originated for the Japanese citizens"; drawing a comparison to Indian reservations, she pointed out that such camps were first established for American Indians. Whether or not one agrees with her conclusion, her points were well taken. And she made an incisive political statement when she wrote, "I believe your shock (that similar injustices could happen to Japanese Americans) came from learning that white Americans did not consider you to be good enough to be part of the oppressor class." But her conclusion reflected what must be her experience—that race supersedes citizenship: "I am an Afro-American and I suppose your letter went to many of us. It probably gave some a good belly-laugh. This may be part of my ignorance, but I am not aware of aid or comfort offered to us by Japanese citizens."

Many people conflated the wartime actions of the Japanese government with the actions of Japanese Americans, holding us responsible for the bombing of Pearl Harbor and hence believing that we got what we deserved: "Remember Pearl Harbor you slant-eyed xxxxx!" "Are you crazy? Don't you know who started the war?" Many who recalled Pearl Harbor obliquely recognized that the hostility was so intense that Japanese Americans were in physical danger. "Call it what you want! A lot of them had their lives saved by the so-called 'concentration camps.'" "Do you people have any idea as to the passion against Japanese in this country in 1942–45? This after the sneak attack on Pearl Harbor. Get off this gravy train—they were lucky to be alive." One woman neatly wrote on flowered stationery, "The Japanese were lucky to be in camps. I'm not a vicious person, but lucky for them I didn't see any Japanese after 'Pearl Harbor' on the streets."

The frequency of such comments prompts one to wonder if people really are unable to distinguish between Americans of Japanese ancestry and Japanese or if people can make the distinction but it just doesn't make a difference. Although we would like to believe that "things are getting better" and injustices like the wholesale incarceration could not happen today, comments such as these seem to prove otherwise. Remarks we received, such as "Tough luck—America first, security first—rights second" and "In war everything is expendable; including some personal freedom," once again surfaced after the September 11, 2001, attacks on the World Trade Center and continue to be heard. While certain things are indeed better, these sentiments remind us that vigilance and determination are still needed to prevent such a travesty of democracy from happening again to any group of people.

# 4  /  The Exhibition
## AMERICA'S CONCENTRATION CAMPS:
## REMEMBERING THE JAPANESE
## AMERICAN EXPERIENCE

The exhibition America's Concentration Camps is presented in this chapter. The contents include the exhibition text panels accompanied by selected photographs and stories that appeared in the original show. The exhibition presented just part of a complex event that occurred during World War II but whose seeds were planted over a century earlier in the racism that permeates America. America's ideals of equality and democracy stand in dramatic contrast to its long history of prejudice and discrimination. There were centers of racial confinement in America, such as slave quarters and American Indian reservations, long before World War II. The World War II concentration camps in America are a specific case of a general tendency in U.S. history to allow racism to override the principles of equality and of liberty and justice for all. The incarceration was unique in that Japanese Americans were free citizens of a democratic nation protected by the Constitution.

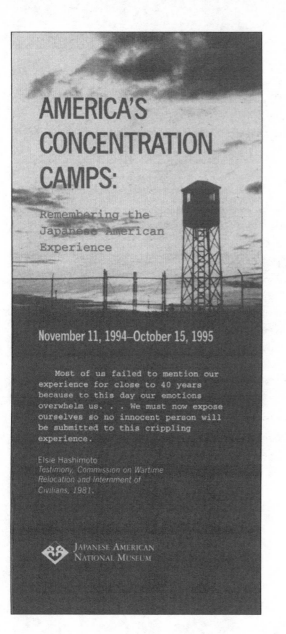

# AMERICA'S CONCENTRATION CAMPS:

Remembering the
Japanese American
Experience

November 11, 1994–October 15, 1995

Most of us failed to mention our
experience for close to 40 years
because to this day our emotions
overwhelm us. . . We must now expose
ourselves so no innocent person will
be submitted to this crippling
experience.

*Elsie Hashimoto*
*Testimony, Commission on Wartime*
*Relocation and Internment of*
*Civilians, 1981.*

JAPANESE AMERICAN
NATIONAL MUSEUM

"I'm for catching
every Japanese in
America, Alaska,
and Hawaii now
and putting them
in concentration
camps...Damn them!
Let's get rid of
them now!"

Congressman
*John Rankin,*

Congressional Record,
December 15, 1941.

# CHRONOLOGY:

**August 10, 1936** President
Franklin D. Roosevelt, in a White
House memorandum, urges
that Japanese citizens or non-
citizens who meet a Japanese
ship "be the first to be placed
in a concentration camp in the
event of trouble."

**November 12, 1941** Fifteen
Japanese American business-
men and commmunity leaders
in Los Angeles' Little Tokyo are
picked up in an F.B.I. raid.
Records and membership lists
for such organizations as the
Japanese Chamber of
Commerce and the Central
Japanese Association are
seized.

**December 7, 1941** After the
attack on Pearl Harbor, local
authorities and the F.B.I. begin
to round up the Issei (first
generation) leadership of the

"They were concen-
tration camps.
They called it
relocation but
they put them in
concentration
camp, and I was
against it. We
were in a period
of emergency, but
it was still the
wrong thing to
do."

President
*Harry S. Truman*

Interview with Merle
Miller, 1961

anese American communities in Hawaii and on
nainland. Within 48 hours, the number arrest·
s 1,291. These men are held under no formal
ges and family members are forbidden to see
m. Most would spend the war years in enemy
n internment camps run by the Justice
artment.

uary 19, 1942 President Roosevelt signs
cutive Order 9066 which allows military authori·
to exclude anyone from anywhere without trial
earings. This order in effect sets the stage for
entire forced removal and incarceration of
anese Americans.

"...it is felt
by a great many
lawyers that under
the Constitution
they (second gen-
eration Japanese
Americans) can't
be kept locked up
in concentration
camps."

President
*Franklin Delano Roosevelt*

Press Conference,
November 21, 1944

military service and dischàrged
many Nisei (second generation)
already serving in the army. In
1943, the U.S. Army reopened
the draft to Nisei.

May 10, 1944 A Federal Grand
Jury issues indictments against
63 Heart Mountain draft resis-
tors. The 63 are found guilty
and sentenced to jail terms on
June 26. They would be granted a pardon on December 24,
1947.

ch 24, 1942 The first of 108 Civilian Exclusion
ders is issued by the Army. All Japanese
ericans living on the West Coast would be
cibly removed and incarcerated in 10 concentra·
n camps from California to Arkansas.

uary 29, 1943 A War Department press release
nounces the registration program for both
ruitment and leave clearance. Two carelessly
rded questions regarding the inmates' loyalty to
e U.S. result in anger and turmoil.

bruary 1, 1943 The 442nd Regimental Combat
am, a segregated unit, is activated. After the
mbing of Pearl Harbor, the U.S. Army re-classi·
d all Japanese Americans as unacceptable for

March 20, 1946 The
last WRA camp, Tule Lake,
closes, culminating "an
incredible mass evacuation
in reverse."

August 10, 1988 HR 422
is signed into law by
President Ronald Reagan.
It provides for individual
reparation payments of
$20,000 to each surviving
internee and a $1.25 billion
education fund among
other provisions.

"I have made a
lot of mistakes
in my life...One is
my part in the
evacuation of the
Japanese from
California in
1942...I don't
think that served
any purpose at
all...We picked
them up and put
them in concentra-
tion camps. That's
the truth of the
matter."

Associate Justice of the
U.S. Supreme Court,
*Tom Clark*

*San Diego Union,*
*July 10, 1966*

Far left: Cover of
exhibition pamphlet.
JANM.

Left: Inside of ex-
hibition pamphlet.
JANM.

## Forced Removal and Incarceration

During World War II, the U.S. government incarcerated more than 120,000 persons of Japanese ancestry, two-thirds of whom were American citizens by birth. Although they were imprisoned for allegedly posing a threat to national security, there was no evidence to support the charge. Americans of Japanese ancestry were placed in what government and military officials, journalists, social commentators, and even two American presidents, Franklin D. Roosevelt and Harry S. Truman, called "concentration camps." This unconstitutional act was carried out without due process of law; it was a result of racism and political deceit at the highest levels of government.

Thousands more Japanese Americans—most of them from Hawai'i, Alaska, the West Coast, and the Southwest—were displaced from their homes and compelled to find other places to live. Although the United States was at war with Germany and Italy as well as Japan, it was only Americans of Japanese ancestry who were subjected to mass removal from their homes and incarceration in concentration camps.

> Has the Gestapo come to America? Have we not risen in righteous anger at Hitler's mistreatment of Jews? Then, is it not incongruous that citizen Americans of Japanese descent should be similarly mistreated and persecuted?
>
> —James Omura, testimony before Select Committee Investigating National Defense Migration, February 23, 1942

"Forced Removal and Incarceration" panel in the exhibition America's Concentration Camps. Photograph by Norman H. Sugimoto.

Mitsu Kawamoto, his brother, and Nob Renge behind barbed wire in Jerome, ca. 1943. Collection of JANM, gift of Masy A. Masuoka (91.139.7).

## Before the War

Japanese began immigrating to Hawai'i and the West Coast in the late 1800s, at the same time that Europeans were immigrating to the East Coast. Unlike their European counterparts, however, Japanese and other Asians were prohibited from becoming naturalized citizens because of their race.

Even as Japanese pioneers were striving to live as Americans, and indeed were contributing to American life, anti-Japanese laws and activities were rampant. Like African American children, Japanese American youngsters were obliged to attend segregated schools. Like the Chinese, Japanese could not own land. Like Mexican Americans, Japanese Americans farmed the land but were excluded from labor unions.

Building on fifty years of anti-Japanese sentiment,

In name, General Benedict Arnold was an American, but at heart he was a traitor. In name, I am not an American, but at heart I am a true American.

—Takao Ozawa, testimony in Supreme Court battle for right of naturalization, 1922

UNCLE SAM'S TROUBLESOME BED FELLOWS

"Uncle Sam's Troublesome Bed Fellows," a cartoon from an 1877 issue of *The Wasp* magazine, shows a disgruntled Uncle Sam kicking a Chinese man and a bearded Mormon out of bed, as American Indian, African American, and Irish men wait their turn. The cartoon illustrates the attitude that has long prevailed in the United States toward racial, ethnic, and religious minorities. Courtesy of Visual Communications (1997.53.1).

Why increase the Sons of Africa, by planting them in America, where we have so fair an opportunity, by excluding all Blacks and Tawneys, of increasing the lovely White?

—Benjamin Franklin, 1751

the U.S. government easily exploited this animosity in order to incarcerate Americans of Japanese ancestry following Japan's attack on Pearl Harbor.

In 1920 Japanese and Filipino workers representing 77 percent of Oahu's workforce went on strike for better wages and working conditions. Invoking Abraham Lincoln as a symbol of freedom and waving American flags, they carried signs reading, "How can we live as Americans on 77 cents?" Collection of JANM, gift of Harry/Kato Mayekawa (2005.26.24).

There were fifty-four sugar plantations in Hawai'i then. Plantations were managed by Americans, Germans and Britishers, below whom were the "poor whites" and Portuguese who were the field overseers. The gap between plantation managers and immigrant workers was wider than that which existed between the lord and peasant during the feudal days in Japan. It was comparable to the relations between the Negro slaves and their masters in the southern part of the United States.

—Yasutaro Soga, ca. 1890

Wonderful Hawai'i, or so I heard.
One look and it seems like Hell.
The manager's the Devil and
His lunas [foremen] are demons.
—"Hole hole bushi," Japanese
plantation workers' song, ca.
1910

When the author's uncle, Kiyoshi Patrick Okura (standing, second from right), attended the University of California, Los Angeles, from 1928 to 1935, Japanese Americans were barred from joining student organizations, so they established the Japanese Bruins Club and their own basketball team. In 1942 the columnist Drew Pearson charged that Okura, who worked for the city of Los Angeles and routinely signed his name K. Patrick Okura, had infiltrated city government by passing himself as Irish. Collection of JANM, gift of Gene Hashiguchi (97.125.1).

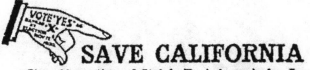

SAVE CALIFORNIA

Stop Absorption of State's Best Acreage by Japanese Through Leases and Evasions of Law.

This advertisement for the California Alien Land Law, which would prevent Japanese from owning land, appeared in October 1920. While the law did not refer to any group, the ad specifically targets the Japanese in an appeal to "Save California." Collection of JANM, courtesy of the *Sacramento Bee* (NRC.1998.188.2).

The author's uncles, Henry Ishizuka and Harry Tanaka, shown as children at the Cawston Ostrich Farm, Pasadena, California, ca. 1922. Collection of JANM, gift of George T. Ishizuka (98.128.1).

Alien hardships
Made bearable by the hope
I hold for my children.
　　—Katsuko, ca. 1920s

The author's grandfather Momota Okura (back row, left) and Okura's five sons, Ben (back row, right), and (front row, left to right) Kiyoshi Patrick, Jimmy Mitsuru, Susumu, and Tsuyoshi. Collection of JANM, courtesy of Frances Etsuko Okura (98.128.235).

America—where
My three sons grow lustily—
More than a wayside stop.
    —Nogiku Itoi, ca. 1920s

## Exclusion Orders

On February 19, 1942, President Franklin D. Roosevelt signed Executive Order 9066, which provided the authority for the forced removal and wholesale incarceration of Japanese Americans. Anticipating the order, nearly 5,000 Japanese Americans moved inland from the West Coast. Soon thereafter, a curfew was imposed, and the army issued 108 civilian exclusion orders, which forced 110,000 Japanese Americans living throughout designated areas in Washington, Oregon, California, and Arizona into concentration camps.

After the exclusion orders were issued, four Supreme Court cases were filed, one each by Fred Korematsu, Gordon Hirabayashi, Mitsuye Endo, and Minoru Yasui, challenging the U.S. government on the legality of detaining people solely on the basis of race.

> Executive Order 9066 was not justified by military necessity. . . . The broad historical causes . . . were race prejudice, war hysteria, and a failure of political leadership.
>
> —*Personal Justice Denied*, Report of the Commission on Wartime Relocation and Internment of Civilians, 1982

WESTERN DEFENSE COMMAND AND FOURTH ARMY
WARTIME CIVIL CONTROL ADMINISTRATION

Presidio of San Francisco, California

May 5, 1942

# INSTRUCTIONS
# TO ALL PERSONS OF
# JAPANESE
## ANCESTRY

### Living in the Following Area:

All of that portion of the City and County of San Francisco, State of California, within that boundary beginning at the intersection of Presidio Avenue and Sutter Street; thence easterly on Sutter Street to Van Ness Avenue; thence southerly on Van Ness Avenue to O'Farrell Street; thence westerly on O'Farrell Street to St. Joseph's Avenue (Calvary Cemetery); thence northerly on St. Joseph's Avenue to Geary Street; thence westerly on Geary Street to Presidio Avenue; thence northerly on Presidio Avenue to the point of beginning.

Pursuant to the provisions of Civilian Exclusion Order No. 41, this Headquarters, dated May 5, 1942, all persons of Japanese ancestry, both alien and non-alien, will be evacuated from the above area by 12 o'clock noon, P. W. T., Monday, May 11, 1942.

No Japanese person living in the above area will be permitted to change residence after 12 o'clock noon, P. W. T., Tuesday, May 5, 1942, without obtaining special permission from the representative of the Commanding General, Northern California Sector, at the Civil Control Station located at:

1530 Buchanan Street,
San Francisco, California.

Such permits will only be granted for the purpose of uniting members of a family, or in cases of grave emergency.

The Civil Control Station is equipped to assist the Japanese population affected by this evacuation in the following ways:

1. Give advice and instructions on the evacuation.
2. Provide services with respect to the management, leasing, sale, storage or other disposition of most kinds of property, such as real estate, business and professional equipment, household goods, boats, automobiles and livestock.
3. Provide temporary residence elsewhere for all Japanese in family groups.
4. Transport persons and a limited amount of clothing and equipment to their new residence.

**The Following Instructions Must Be Observed:**

1. A responsible member of each family, preferably the head of the family, or the person in whose name most of the property is held, and each individual living alone, will report to the Civil Control Station to receive further instructions. This must be done between 8:00 A. M. and 5:00 P. M. on Wednesday, May 6, 1942, or between 8:00 A. M. and 5:00 P. M. on Thursday, May 7, 1942.
2. Evacuees must carry with them on departure for the Assembly Center, the following property:
   (a) Bedding and linens (no mattress) for each member of the family;
   (b) Toilet articles for each member of the family;
   (c) Extra clothing for each member of the family;
   (d) Sufficient knives, forks, spoons, plates, bowls and cups for each member of the family;
   (e) Essential personal effects for each member of the family.

All items carried will be securely packaged, tied and plainly marked with the name of the owner and numbered in accordance with instructions obtained at the Civil Control Station. The size and number of packages is limited to that which can be carried by the individual or family group.

3. No pets of any kind will be permitted.
4. No personal items and no household goods will be shipped to the Assembly Center.
5. The United States Government through its agencies will provide for the storage, at the sole risk of the owner, of the more substantial household items, such as iceboxes, washing machines, pianos and other heavy furniture. Cooking utensils and other small items will be accepted for storage if crated, packed and plainly marked with the name and address of the owner. Only one name and address will be used by a given family.
6. Each family, and individual living alone, will be furnished transportation to the Assembly Center or will be authorized to travel by private automobile in a supervised group. All instructions pertaining to the movement will be obtained at the Civil Control Station.

**Go to the Civil Control Station between the hours of 8:00 A. M. and 5:00 P. M., Wednesday, May 6, 1942, or between the hours of 8:00 A. M. and 5:00 P. M., Thursday, May 7, 1942, to receive further instructions.**

J. L. DeWITT
Lieutenant General, U. S. Army
Commanding

SEE CIVILIAN EXCLUSION ORDER NO. 41

The details of the exclusion orders are important to note. In this one, only six days were allowed for people of Japanese ancestry to dispose of all belongings and prepare for an indefinite leave. The reference to "all persons of Japanese ancestry both alien and non-alien" mitigated the fact that this order applied to U.S. citizens. They were instructed to take their own bedding, linen, eating utensils, and clothing but were "limited to that which can be carried." Collection of JANM, gift of Kiyoshi Toi (92.94.1).

## The Process of Incarceration

The U.S. government's process of removing thousands of people from their homes and incarcerating them in camps was exceedingly complex. It began even before the issuing of Executive Order 9066, immediately after Pearl Harbor was bombed, with the arrest of hundreds of Issei who were primarily community leaders. These Issei, along with selected German and Italian nationals, were arrested and detained in internment camps run by the U.S. Justice Department.

The author's grandfather Momota Okura (first row, fourth from left) was sent to Justice Department internment camps in Fort Missoula, Montana; Fort Sill, Oklahoma; Camp Livingston, Louisiana; and Santa Fe, New Mexico, during a two-year period before being allowed to join his family in the WRA camp in Jerome, Arkansas. Courtesy of Frances Etsuko Okura.

The Santa Anita race track in California was used as an assembly center from March 27 to October 7, 1942. Horse stalls were used as living quarters. At its peak, the center held 18,719 men, women, and children. Collection of JANM, gift of George Ishizuka (98.128.51).

Executive Order 9066 mandated that people of Japanese ancestry living in areas designated by the military's Western Defense Command, which essentially constituted America's entire West Coast, were subjected to a curfew and restriction of movement. They were forced to quickly dispose of their homes, businesses, and belongings and report to so-called assembly centers. These centers were hastily converted facilities such as fairgrounds and race tracks, where families were held from one to seven months.

## Misleading Terminology

The process of incarceration was couched in words and expressions that hid the government's real intent:

> An "Assembly Center" was a euphemism for a prison . . . so-called "Relocation Centers," a euphemism for concentration camps.
>
> —Supreme Court Justice Owen J. Roberts, dissenting opinion, *Korematsu v. U.S.*, December 18, 1944

"evacuation" = exclusion, forced removal

"relocation" = incarceration in camps; also used after release from camp

"non-aliens" = U.S. citizens of Japanese ancestry

"civilian exclusion orders" = detention orders

"any or all persons" = primarily persons of Japanese ancestry

"may be excluded" = evicted from one's home

"relocation center" = concentration camp

"assembly center" = detention facility

"native American aliens" = citizens who, under pressure, renounced U.S. citizenship

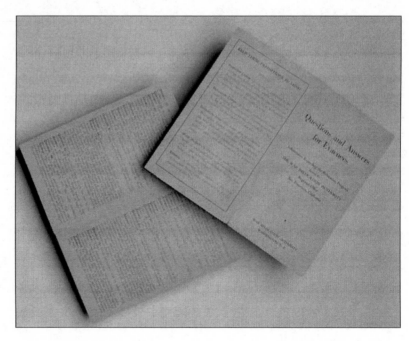

In this pamphlet produced by the War Relocation Authority, "assembly center" is defined as "a convenient gathering point"; a "relocation center" is called a "pioneer community." Collection of JANM, courtesy of the Francis Hayashi Family (96.164.1).

## Japanese Latin American Hostages

From 1942 to 1945, the U.S. government orchestrated the forcible deportation of over 2,260 persons of Japanese ancestry from thirteen Latin American countries. The deportees were incarcerated in the United States and to be used by the U.S. government as hostages in exchange for Americans held by Japan. About 80 percent of the deportees were from Peru.

Over five hundred Japanese Peruvians were included in two prisoner-of-war exchanges that took place in 1942 and 1943. The remaining Japanese Latin Americans continued to be incarcerated in the United States. After the war, they were considered "illegal aliens," but the Peruvian government refused to readmit any Japanese Peruvians, even those who were Peruvian citizens.

As a result, hundreds of Japanese Peruvians were deported to war-devastated Japan, a country many had never visited and with which

Japanese Peruvian Girl Scouts in Crystal City. Collection of JANM, gift of Dr. Sumi Shimatsu (97.89.5).

most had no ties. Three hundred remained in the United States and fought deportation through the courts. Eventually, about one hundred Japanese Peruvians were allowed to return to Peru.

In the exhibition, a map titled "The Process of Incarceration" showed that Japanese from as far away as Alaska and Hawaiʻi (neither of which were states at the time) and even South America were sent to camps in the United States. JANM. Photograph by Norman H. Sugimoto.

## Hawai'i's Japanese Americans

There were more Americans of Japanese ancestry in Hawai'i than in the entire continental United States. If Japanese Americans posed an actual threat to national security, all Japanese Americans in Hawai'i, which had been attacked by Japan, would also have been incarcerated. Yet there was no mass incarceration in Hawai'i, largely because Hawai'i's economy was highly dependent on its Japanese American labor force.

Instead, selected Japanese Americans were held in immigration stations, jails, and military facilities on all the islands. Two camps—Sand Island and Honouliuli detention camps on Oahu—were established in Hawai'i. Eventually, over eleven hundred Japanese Americans from Hawai'i were sent to mainland camps. In addition to those detained in Hawai'i and shipped to mainland camps, an estimated fifteen hundred Japanese Americans living near military installations were evicted from their homes. Mostly farmers, they were allowed to work their land from 6 A.M. to 6 P.M. but were forced to find housing elsewhere.

## Alaska's Japanese Americans

About 150 Japanese were taken from their homes in Alaska. Like their mainland counterparts, men were picked up first and confined in Justice Department internment camps. Their families were initially interned in Alaska and then airlifted to the state of Washington. From there they were taken to the concentration camp in Minidoka, Idaho.

On December 7, 1941, we were the only Japanese American family in Kodiak, Alaska. In a short time my father and two uncles were arrested and put in concentration camps in the United States. I have never seen my father since.

—Ewan Yoshida, testimony before Commission on Wartime Relocation and Internment of Civilians, Los Angeles, August 1981

## America's Concentration Camps

As a teenage participant in this mass exodus I, like others, went along into confinement. . . . In our immaturity and naiveté, many of us who were American citizens believed that this, under the circumstances, was the only way to prove our loyalty.

—Michi Nishiura Weglyn, former internee, Gila River, 1976

After months of being shuffled through assembly centers and other detention centers, over 100,000 men, women, and children of Japanese ancestry found themselves behind barbed wire in concentration camps located in some of the most desolate areas of the United States. The incarceration lasted from a few months to four and a half years.

Life in the camps varied, depending on the individual camp, its administration, the time period, and the internee's age, gender, personality, and political convictions. For the most part, people tried to make the best life they could under extraordinary circumstances. But

Banners mark the Heart Mountain and Tule Lake camp clusters in the exhibition America's Concentration Camps: Remembering the Japanese American Experience. Photograph by Norman H. Sugimoto.

they could never forget that the camps were essentially prisons, in most cases guarded by sentries in watchtowers equipped with searchlights and machine guns. As one inmate said, "If it was for our protection, why did the guns point inward, rather than outward?"

## Life behind Barbed Wire

Life in the camps meant lack of privacy, poor food, and a need to adjust to a strange and isolated place. But most people did their best to lead normal lives under abnormal conditions. Through an ironic combination of the inmates' own efforts and the paternalism of the administration, each camp became a self-contained colony. In time, each had its own newspaper, school, religious institutions, and hospital. Yet life was anything but normal.

> This is the story of an act unprecedented in American history both in itself and in its implications: the evacuation of more than 70,000 citizens, charged with no crime, into concentration camps by presidential fiat.
> —Norman Thomas, July 1942

As U.S. citizens, Japanese American males were eligible for the draft, and many served in the U.S. Army. However, after Pearl Harbor, Nisei were reclassified as "enemy aliens," making them unacceptable for military service, and many were summarily discharged from the army. In 1943 the army established a segregated combat unit to be made up of Nisei soldiers. Almost ten thousand Japanese American men from Hawai'i and over twelve hundred from the mainland volunteered for the all-Nisei 442nd Regimental Combat Team. While their parents were incarcerated in concentration camps on the mainland and subjected to martial law in Hawai'i, Japanese American soldiers fought and died for their country.

Men being inducted into the U.S. Army at Manzanar. Collection of JANM, gift of Grace and George Izumi (94.182.11).

I know that you boys and your families have more reason than some of the rest of us to know that this country, which is now calling you to service, is not a perfect country. It is not a country where everyone is equal and treated equally. It is not a country which is free from prejudice. But I am sure that you boys know that with all its faults this country is the best on the face of the earth.

—Byron Ver Ploeg, project attorney, speech to Heart Mountain draftees, *Heart Mountain Sentinel,* July 22, 1944

In 1944, I was inducted into the U.S. Army. The loyal American part of me welcomed the chance to be an American soldier with an opportunity to show my loyalty. The more rational part of me recognized the irony of being inducted from a concentration camp where my parents were still incarcerated.

—Junji Kumamoto, Ph.D., testimony before Commission on Wartime Relocation and Internment of Civilians, Los Angeles, August 1981

Women's Army Corps (WAC) volunteer in Rohwer. Collection of JANM, gift of the Maruyama Family (93.176.1).

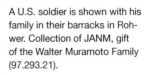

A U.S. soldier is shown with his family in their barracks in Rohwer. Collection of JANM, gift of the Walter Muramoto Family (97.293.21).

The 100th Infantry Battalion/442nd Regimental Combat Team, a segregated Japanese American unit of the U.S. Army, accomplished and endured much during the war:

7 major campaigns in Europe
7 Presidential Unit Citations
9,486 casualties
18,143 individual decorations, including:
    1 Congressional Medal of Honor
    52 Distinguished Service Crosses
    1 Distinguished Service Medal
    560 Silver Stars, with 28 Oak Leaf Clusters representing second awards
    22 Legion of Merit Medals
    Approximately 4,000 Bronze Stars, with about 1,200 Oak Leaf Clusters representing second awards
    Approximately 3,600 Purple Hearts, including 500 Oak Leaf Clusters
    15 Soldier's Medals
    12 French Croix de Guerre, with two Palms representing second awards
    2 Italian Crosses for Military Merit
    2 Italian Medals for Military Valor

## Amache

Panoramic view of Granada, more commonly called Amache. Collection of JANM, gift of Minoru Tonai (98.195.1).

Official name: Granada Relocation Center

Location: Prowers County, Colorado

Dates of operation: August 27, 1942, to October 15, 1945

Peak population: 7,318

Project area: 10,500 acres

Number of draft-age males inducted into the armed forces: 494

Number of births: 415

Number of deaths: 106

Number of weddings: 164

Number of people segregated to Tule Lake, California: 215

Although Japan was at war with the United States, the Japanese government sent relief goods of soy sauce and tea to the incarcerated Americans of Japanese descent through the International Red Cross. This shipment reached Amache in April 1944. Collection of JANM, gift of Nishizaki Family (94.194.7).

PAGE 4    SAN FRANCISCO CHRONICLE, SUNDAY, FEB. 27, 1944    CCCCAA

## ELEVEN DEMANDS PRESENTED TO WRA
# Nisei Ask Right to Go Anywhere in U. S.

WASHINGTON, Feb. 26 (P) — Japanese-Americans in the relocation center at Granada, Colo., have presented 11 demands on the War Relocation Authority, including a plea that they be given freedom to live and travel anywhere in the United States, Dillon S. Myer, WRA Director, disclosed today.

With little comment aside from a statement that he would answer the Japanese-Americans' queries "with the best information available" and turn the others over to proper Government agencies, Myer made public a letter from the center's community council.

Asking that the camp occupants be restored their full rights as United States citizens, the letter said draft-age evacuee Americans of Japanese ancestry had been responding to the call for military service and civilian responsibility to aid the war effort.

These requests were made of Myer:

1—That equal opportunity for service and advancement in all branches in the armed forces and Japanese - American draftees solely on the basis of individual merit and qualification.

2—That Japanese-American service men who are called to the colors hereafter be co-mingled with citizens of other racial extractions and not be assigned to segregated units.

3—That an evacuee's right to travel and live wherever he chooses within any of the 48 States and territories of the United States, on the same basis as any other American citizen or residents, be restored without delay.

4—That all evacuees be accorded all the rights and privileges which the Constitution gives them.

5—That any resettlement policy of the evacuees still remaining in the centers be coupled with adequate government protection and the economic means to start life anew.

6—That clarification be made regarding voting and residenceship status of Japanese-Americans who become of age in the centers.

7—That the right to become naturalized citizens of the United States be extended to the alien Japanese.

8—That pending complete resettlement, relocation centers be preserved and evacuees remaining therein be accorded treatment befitting loyal Americans and law-abiding residents and that adequate wages be paid them scaled according to Army standards.

9—That immediate and more vigorous effort be made by the Government toward enlightening the "misinformed" American public

with truth regarding the Japanese in America, and that the factual difference between the people of Japanese extraction who are loyal citizens and law abiding residents of this country and the Japanese people in Japan be clearly presented.

10—That students of Japanese ancestry be freely admitted to all the schools on the same basis with students of any other extraction.

11—That the United States Government establish adequate precautionary measures so that the "sad" experiences of evacuation be never again repeated either with the Japanese or with any other group because of race, color or creed.

The letter concluded with the statement that the requests were being made "in the hope that our democracy may be made more perfect for the benefit of everyone."

On February 27, 1944, the *San Francisco Chronicle* reported on eleven demands made by inmates in Amache. Among other things, the prisoners asked for immediate and more vigorous efforts by the U.S. government to enlighten the American public regarding the truth about Japanese in America, that all constitutional rights and privileges be reinstituted, and that the United States government establish adequate precautionary measures so that wrongful incarceration never again be repeated with any group because of race, color, or creed. Reprinted with permission of the *San Francisco Chronicle*. Collection of JANM, gift of the American Friends Service Committee (94.122.2A).

Chizuyo Kanazawa with (left to right) her husband, James, who volunteered for the army from Amache, and their sons Jay and Keiji. They are shown in Chicago after being released from camp in 1944. Collection of JANM, gift of Mary N. Karasawa (96.24.13).

Chizuyo Kanazawa was the mother of two young boys when her family was forced to leave its home in Los Angeles. In this journal entry, she gives us a rare glimpse of the frightful days before the exclusion: "Saturday, March 21, 1942. Downtown—mob of shoppers—future evacuees. Looks of despair. Some state of hysteria. Lots of good-byes for duration with heart-touching scenes on street. Unbelievable condition. The scene cannot be erased from my mind."

In Amache, Mrs. Kanazawa helped form the Women's Federation, made up of four elected representatives from each block. The group's statement of purpose declares that the Women's Federation "attempts to be the mouthpiece of women in camp and make demands and dissatisfactions known to the administration. It is an organization which attempts to better camp conditions and present points men councilmen think superfluous."

## Crystal City

Aerial view of Crystal City. Collection of JANM, gift of the Joe Ando Family (98.194.1).

Official name: Crystal City, Texas Internment Center

Location: Crystal City, Zavala County, Texas

Dates of operation: December 12, 1942, to December 1947

Peak population: 3,374 (2,371 persons of Japanese descent, 997 Germans, and 6 Italians)

Project area: 290 acres

Number of births: 153

Number of deaths: 17

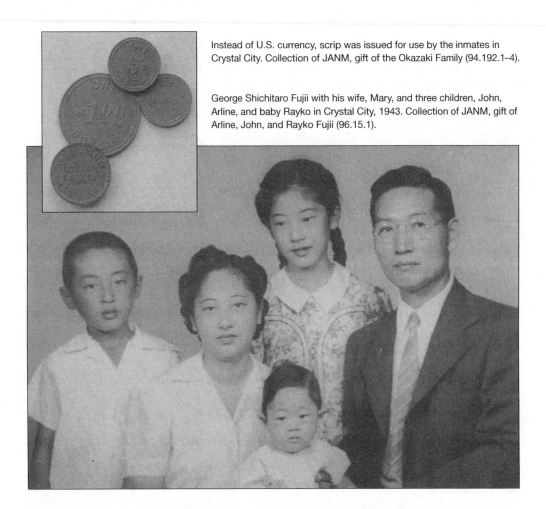

Instead of U.S. currency, scrip was issued for use by the inmates in Crystal City. Collection of JANM, gift of the Okazaki Family (94.192.1–4).

George Shichitaro Fujii with his wife, Mary, and three children, John, Arline, and baby Rayko in Crystal City, 1943. Collection of JANM, gift of Arline, John, and Rayko Fujii (96.15.1).

George Shichitaro Fujii was an interpreter for a rice importer when he immigrated to the United States in 1924 at the age of twenty-four. In 1942, he was taken from his home and family in Seattle and placed in a Justice Department internment camp in Bismarck, North Dakota. Soon thereafter, his wife, son, and daughter were incarcerated in Tule Lake, California. Two and a half years later, they were reunited in Crystal City.

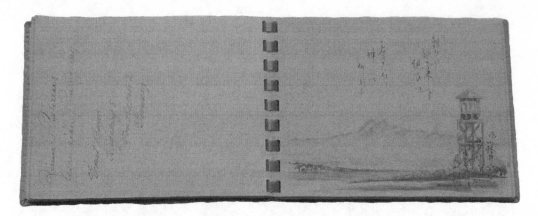

George Fujii's family autograph book. Collection of JANM, gift of Dr. Arline Fujii McCord (94.202.1).

The family saved an autograph book containing good wishes, poems, and names and addresses from fellow inmates throughout Fujii's incarceration. Reflecting the multinational character of Crystal City, the left-hand page in the photograph shows autographs from a person from Paraguay and another from Germany. The right-hand page contains a poem from an inmate in Lordsburg, New Mexico, in which the writer wishes Fujii the best of luck in the future as they remember the mornings and evenings of their shared past.

# Gila River

Panoramic view of Gila River. Collection of JANM, gift of Sachio J. Takata, M.D. (97.44.18).

Official name: Gila River Relocation Center
Location: Pinal County, Arizona
Dates of operation: July 20, 1942, to September 28, 1945 (Canal Camp), and to November 10, 1945 (Butte Camp)
Peak population: 13,348
Project area: 16,000 acres
Number of draft-age males inducted into the armed forces: 487
Number of births: 662
Number of deaths: 221
Number of weddings: 214
Number of people segregated to Tule Lake, California: 2,005

Michiko Nishiura Weglyn was fifteen years old when she entered the Gila River camp. Ironically, within the confines of an American concentration camp, she was as "all-American" as one could be. She was head of the Girl's League in high school, played the violin, and even received a scholastic award from the American Legion upon her graduation. Thirty-four years later, Weglyn wrote *Years of Infamy: The Untold Story of America's Concentration Camps,* one of the most important books on the subject. In the preface, she wrote, "I hope this uniquely American story will serve as a reminder to all those who cherish their liberties of the very fragility of their rights . . . and as a warning that they who say that it can never happen again are probably wrong."

First Lady Eleanor Roosevelt and Dillon S. Myer, director of the War Relocation Authority, visiting Gila River, 1943. Collection of JANM, gift of Michi and Walter M. Weglyn (94.170.7).

Michiko Nishiura Weglyn in Gila River. Collection of JANM, gift of Michi and Walter M. Weglyn (94.170.6).

## Heart Mountain

Official name: Heart Mountain Relocation Center
Location: Northwestern Wyoming
Dates of operation: August 12, 1942, to November 10, 1945
Peak population: 10,767
Project area: 46,000 acres
Number of draft-age males inducted into the armed forces: 385
Number of births: 550
Number of deaths: 182
Number of weddings: 223
Number of people segregated to Tule Lake, California: 988

An inmate wears his letterman sweater behind barbed wire in Heart Mountain. Collection of JANM, gift of Kimie Nagai (92.125.23).

Frank Emi (right) and Guntaro Kubota, members of the Fair Play Committee in Heart Mountain, 1944. Gift of Frank S. Emi (96.109.28).

Frank Emi was one of the leaders of the Heart Mountain Fair Play Committee, the largest organized resistance to the draft in any of the camps. Citing the American principles of equality and justice, the FPC declared that only when all constitutional rights and freedoms were restored could the government ask men to fight and die for their country:

> We, the members of the FPC, are not afraid to go to war. . . . We would gladly sacrifice our lives to protect and uphold the princi-

In 1944, a total of eighty-five men from Heart Mountain were convicted of draft resistance in two trials. In December 1947, all Japanese American draft resisters were issued a pardon by President Truman. Collection of JANM, gift of Frank S. Emi (96.109.27).

ples and ideals of our country as set forth in the Constitution. . . . But have we been given such freedom, such liberty, such justice, such protection? NO!! . . . And then, without rectification of the injustices committed against us nor without restoration of our rights as guaranteed by the Constitution, we are ordered to join the Army through discriminatory procedures into a segregated combat unit! The FPC believes that unless such actions are opposed NOW, and steps taken to remedy such injustices and discrimination immediately, the future of all minorities and the future of this democratic nation is in danger.

Emi and the other FPC members were arrested and charged with conspiracy to counsel, aid, and abet violation of the Selective Service Act.

## Jerome

Official name: Jerome Relocation Center

Location: Drew and Chicot Counties, southeastern Arkansas

Dates of operation: October 6, 1942 to June 30, 1944

Peak population: 8,497

Project area: 10,000 acres

Number of draft-age males inducted into the armed forces: 52

Number of births: 239

Number of deaths: 76

Number of weddings: 103

Number of people segregated to Tule Lake, California: 2,147

Barracks in Jerome. Collection of JANM, gift of Arthur S. Fujikawa (98.94.13).

Yuri Nakahara Kochiyama and her Sunday school students in Jerome. Collection of JANM, gift of Yuri Kochiyama (96.42.6).

Yuri Nakahara Kochiyama was a young Sunday school teacher in San Pedro when she and her family were sent to the Santa Anita Assembly Center and then to Jerome in Arkansas. While in Santa Anita, Kochiyama began her lifelong commitment to social change and human-rights advocacy.

She organized her Sunday school class to correspond with Nisei soldiers in the military to keep up their morale. Within two years, the list of five soldiers had expanded to thirteen thousand. The young correspondents called themselves the "Crusaders." When they were dispersed to different camps, they kept up the effort. In Jerome, the Crusaders were led by Yuri's energy and enthusiasm, and the group grew especially large. Soon there were Junior Crusaders, of junior high school age, and Junior Junior Crusaders, made up of children in grammar school.

Yuri Nakahara Kochiyama's folders bearing the names of thirteen thousand Nisei soldiers. The author's uncle, Private Susumu Okura of the U.S. Army, was killed in battle at the age of nineteen. He is listed in a folder and noted as deceased. Mae Shizuko (Okura) Komatsu and Frances Etsuko Okura, aunts of the author, were members of Kochiyama's Junior and Junior Junior Crusaders. Collection of JANM, gift of Yuri Kochiyama (94.144.2).

A Christmas greeting to the Crusaders from Captain S. Takahashi. Collection of JANM, gift of Yuri Kochiyama (94.144.1).

# Manzanar

Official name: Manzanar Relocation Center

Location: Inyo County, California

Dates of operation: June 1, 1942, to November 21, 1945

Peak population: 10,046

Project area: 60,000 acres

Number of draft-age males inducted into the armed forces: 174

Number of births: 541

Number of deaths: 146

Number of weddings: 188

Number of people segregated to Tule Lake, California: 2,165

Children at Manzanar salute the American flag the old way. Collection of JANM, gift of Charles and Lois Ferguson (94.180.52).

Charles and Lois Ferguson at Merritt Park, a garden designed and built by Kuichiro Nishi, the author's grandfather, in Manzanar. Collection of JANM, gift of Charles and Lois Ferguson (94.180.41).

Lois Ferguson (third from left) and student teachers in Manzanar. Collection of JANM, gift of Charles and Lois Ferguson (94.180.21).

Lois Ferguson was a teacher in Manzanar. Her husband, Charles, was director of adult education. At the camp, she wrote letters to friends about Manzanar. In a letter dated September 19, 1942, she said:

> You don't have to live here long to discover that something you strongly suspicioned [*sic*] before you entered is true—only the rosier side of our treatment of the Japanese goes to the press. Articles such as Jim Marshall's in an Aug. issue of "Colliers," in which he ends up saying Americans need feel nothing but pride over the Japanese Relocation Camps, are definitely misleading, to say the least. True, we don't beat them physically or starve them or anything as obviously brutal as all that, but Manzanar is no Utopia, and it is supposed to be one of the best of the camps.

In another letter, she wrote about the Manzanar riot of December 6, 1942, which resulted in two deaths and many injured. She concluded, "I am convinced that the vast majority of Japanese (both American citizens and alien) are still decidedly loyal to the U.S. even in spite of being denied all their rights of life, liberty and the pursuit of happiness. I'm wondering how the rest of us could have stood the test under similar circumstances."

## Minidoka

View of Minidoka. Photograph, United States Bureau of Reclamation. Courtesy of Phil Taijitsu Nash (NRC 1998.249.6).

Official name: Minidoka Relocation Center

Location: Jerome County, south-central Idaho

Dates of operation: August 10, 1942, to October 28, 1945

Peak population: 9,397

Project area: 33,000 acres

Number of draft-age males inducted into the armed forces: 594

Number of births: 489

Number of deaths: 193

Number of weddings: 155

Number of people segregated to Tule Lake, California: 335

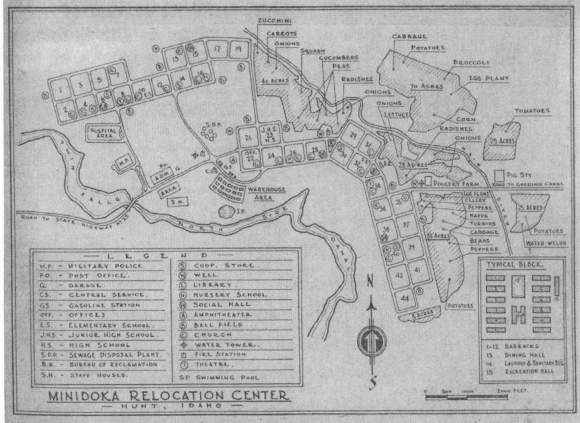

MAP OF MINIDOKA RELOCATION CENTER

A birdseye view of the Minidoka Relocation Project. Shaped like a half moon, it is approximately three miles long. About 8500 people are living in the temporary barracks.

Hand-drawn map of Minidoka. Collection of JANM, gift of the Maruyama Family (93.176.1).

Baggage being unloaded at Minidoka. Photograph, United States Bureau of Reclamation. Courtesy of Phil Taijitsu Nash (NRC 1998.249.3).

When the United States entered the war, Norio Mitsuoka was a member of the U.S. Army Air Corps. On February 17, 1943, Mitsuoka, like many other Japanese American soldiers, was administratively discharged, relieved from active duty, and sent home. When his mother learned that her son had joined the U.S. Army, she had a *senninbari* made for him.

A *senninbari* is made up of a thousand knotted stitches and is presented to a soldier when he goes off to war. Each stitch is sewn by a different woman and carries her hopes for the soldier's well-being. Mitsuoka took the *senninbari* to Minidoka with him.

The *senninbari* given to Norio Mitsuoko by his mother. Collection of JANM, gift of Norio Mitsuoka (94.113.2).

# Poston

Panoramic view of Poston. Collection of Toshiye C. and Donald H. Estes (NRC 2004.242.1).

Official name: Colorado River Relocation Center

Location: Yuma County, Arizona

Dates of operation: May 8, 1942 to November 28, 1945 (Unit I); to September 29, 1945 (Unit II); to September 29, 1945 (Unit III)

Peak population: 17,814

Project area: 71,000 acres

Number of draft-age males inducted into the armed forces: 611

Number of births: 793

Number of deaths: 300

Number of weddings: 285

Number of people segregated to Tule Lake, California: 1,429

"Out of the Desert" album compiled by Poston high-school students, 1942–43. Collection of JANM, gift of Mrs. Etsu Mineta Masaoka (93.109.1)

A page from "Out of the Desert." Collection of JANM, gift of Mrs. Etsu Mineta Masaoka (93.109.1).

"Out of the Desert" is an album of poems, essays, and artwork composed primarily by high-school students in Unit I, one of the three camps that made up Poston, during the winter of 1942–43. Several albums were made. The intent of the project was to give the albums to high schools around the nation so the incarcerated students could develop pen-pal relationships with their peers. However, the authorities did not allow the albums to circulate. The first page of "Out of the Desert" reads:

> To Our Fellow Americans,
> Deep from out this lonely desert's vastness,
> We, the Japanese American Youth,
> Innocent of wrong,
> Firm in our Hope and our Faith,
> Cherishing forever the ideals of our Native Land,
> Striving to build in the wilderness,
> Struggling to build our Destiny,
> Extend to you . . .
> our Fellowship.

# Rohwer

View of Rohwer. Collection of JANM, gift of the Walter Muramoto Family (97.292.15D).

Official name: Rohwer Relocation Center

Location: Desha County, southeastern Arkansas

Dates of operation: September 18, 1942, to November 30, 1945

Peak population: 8,475

Project area: 10,000 acres

Number of draft-age males inducted into the armed forces: 274

Number of births: 418

Number of deaths: 168

Number of weddings: 153

Number of people segregated to Tule Lake, California: 1,430

Inmates leaving Rohwer as others bid farewell. Collection of JANM, gift of Walter Muramoto Family (97.293.23).

Drawing of Gihachi Yamashita in scrapbook that he kept through his detention in various Justice Department internment camps. Collection of JANM, gift of the Gihachi and Tsugio Yamashita Family (94.166.29).

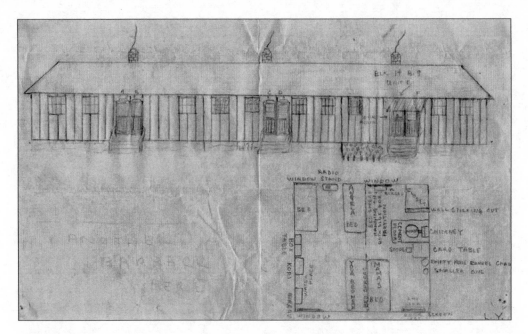

Drawing of the family's barracks compartment in Rohwer sent to Gihachi Yamashita by his daughter Lillian, October 1942. Collection of JANM, gift of Gihachi and Tsugio Yamashita Family (94.166.24).

Gihachi Yamashita was born in 1889 and was fifty-two years old when he was arrested in the early morning of December 8, 1941. One of his later diary entries, translated here, recalls that night:

January 22, 1942
December 8, 1941, one-thirty in the morning. I can never forget that day. Two FBI agents knocked me out of my bed and took me to the police station for some questioning. After four days in the Lincoln Heights jail, I was transferred to the county jail on the 12th and I have been here ever since.

In Yamashita's album, this poem by a fellow inmate reveals the emotions of fathers separated from their families:

On my first day at the mess hall
I came upon the true meaning of life.
At the bottom of my darkness
I saw the reflection of my wife and child.
  —Taro Suma, Camp Livingston, 1943

# Topaz

Panoramic view of Topaz. Collection of JANM, gift of Fred H. and Masa Moriguchi.

Official name: Central Utah Relocation Center

Location: Millard County, Utah

Dates of operation: September 11, 1942, to October 31, 1945

Peak population: 8,130

Project area: 19,000 acres

Number of draft-age males inducted into the armed forces: 472

Number of births: 384

Number of deaths: 139

Number of weddings: 136

Number of people segregated to Tule Lake, California: 1,459

The artist Chiura Obata documented life in camp through several hundred sketches. This one memorializes the murder of an inmate, Hatsuki Wakasa, on April 11, 1943. The first reports stated that the elderly man, who had served the U.S. Army as a civilian cooking instructor during World War I, was attempting to crawl through the fence. However, later investigation by the government found that this account was part of a coverup initiated by the army officer in charge. Collection of JANM, estate of Chiura Obata (22.1992.7).

Opposite page: Cover of *Trek,* a camp literary and artistic publication produced in Topaz. Collection of JANM, gift of John A. Trice (94.28.4).

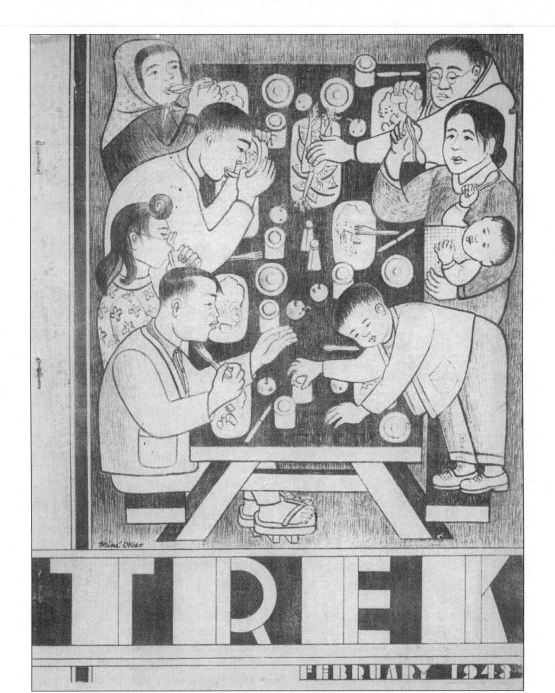

TREK

FEBRUARY 1943

*Trek* was the literary and artistic publication created by the inmates in Topaz. Entries ranged from the eloquent to the sarcastic to the downright funny. In the first issue, in December 1942, one Globularius Schraubi, M.A., wrote, "What concerns us at the moment is the alingual status of Japa-Mericans in the Areas into which they were recently imported and where they are now concentrated . . . otherwise known as Little Nip Pons or Nip Pounds—not that they are shelters for nipping canines."

"In Topaz," a poem by Toyo Suyemoto, appeared in the second issue, in February 1943:

Can this hard earth break wide
The stiff stillness of snow
And yield me promise that
This is not always so?

On the last page of the last issue, June 1943, Jim Yamada wrote, "Now that our return to normal life is imminent, we find that the impressions of evacuation most sharply etched in our mind are not the kind we thought we would remember six months ago. The last few months have smoothed over a lot of the sharp edges of our original anger and bitterness, and now we see more of the light as well as the shadows."

## Tule Lake

Inmates line up outside a mess hall in Tule Lake. Collection of JANM, gift of Yukio Nakamura (93.92.1).

Official name: Tule Lake Relocation Center

Location: Klamath Falls Basin, Northern California

Dates of operation: May 27, 1942, to March 20, 1946; designated a segregation
center on July 15, 1943

Peak population: 18,789

Project area: 7,400 acres

Number of draft-age males inducted into the armed forces: 57

Number of births: 1,490

Number of deaths: 331

Number of weddings: 499

Security officers drag an inmate in Tule Lake. Collection of JANM, gift of Michi Weglyn (96.33.3).

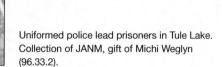

Uniformed police lead prisoners in Tule Lake. Collection of JANM, gift of Michi Weglyn (96.33.2).

Tule Lake was transformed into a "segregation center" to isolate the so-called loyal inmates from the disloyal, categories based on a poorly conceived and executed questionnaire. A stockade held several hundred inmates. Regardless of inmates' "loyalty" status, they were denied permission to resettle out of the camp. The partial self-government system established in other centers was not allowed at Tule Lake.

Masako Koga Murakami is at far right in this photo of children in front of a barracks in Tule Lake. Collection of JANM, gift of Masako Iwawaki Koga (96.14.10).

Masako Koga Murakami was seven years old when she was incarcerated in Gila River in 1942. Her parents answered "no" to the infamous question 27, which asked if men were willing to serve in the U.S. armed forces, and question 28, which asked even Issei who were not allowed to become U.S. citizens to swear allegiance to the United States and forswear allegiance to Japan. Masako and her family were considered "disloyal" and sent to Tule Lake.

## The Struggle for Redress

You ask me what I think would be a proper reparation for the damages I suffered? I want to be returned to age 25, where I can live life the way I could have lived.

—Shigeo Nishimura, testimony before Commission on Wartime Relocation and Internment of Civilians, Los Angeles, August 1981

The roots of the redress movement lay in the camps themselves, with the inmates who demonstrated, conducted strikes, wrote letters, and otherwise challenged the incarceration. While there was some measure of compensation and apology in the years immediately following the war, the massive effort by the Japanese American community to seek an official apology and monetary damages for the incarceration began in earnest in the 1970s.

Various routes leading toward the same goal were vigorously pursued across the country. Documents were uncovered showing that the U.S. government had

The National Coalition for Redress/Reparations (NCRR), the National Committee for Redress of the Japanese American Citizens League (JACL), and the National Council for Japanese American Redress (NCJAR) were the three major organizations campaigning for redress from the U.S. government. Collection of JANM, gift of Janice Iwanaga Yen (98.316.5).

THE WHITE HOUSE
WASHINGTON

A monetary sum and words alone cannot restore lost years or erase painful memories; neither can they fully convey our Nation's resolve to rectify injustice and to uphold the rights of individuals. We can never fully right the wrongs of the past. But we can take a clear stand for justice and recognize that serious injustices were done to Japanese Americans during World War II.

In enacting a law calling for restitution and offering a sincere apology, your fellow Americans have, in a very real sense, renewed their traditional commitment to the ideals of freedom, equality, and justice. You and your family have our best wishes for the future.

Sincerely,

GEORGE BUSH
PRESIDENT OF THE UNITED STATES

OCTOBER 1990

A letter of apology from President George H. W. Bush to survivors of America's concentration camps after the campaign for redress was won. Collection of JANM, gift of Bob and Rumi Uragami (93.179.1).

suppressed, altered, and destroyed evidence in the cases challenging the legality of the incarceration. This led to the vacating of the convictions of Fred Korematsu, Gordon Hirabayashi, and Minoru Yasui for having resisted the curfew and the exclusion orders. A class-action suit against the United States was also filed. Ultimately, these efforts led to the passage of the Civil Liberties Act of 1988, which provided an apology from the U.S. government and token monetary compensation to the existing survivors of America's concentration camps.

## The Past as Present

Walking away from the camp, I wondered if we will someday learn how to cross the barbed wire borders in our lives, and . . . help free everyone else who continues to be confined in their concentration camps.

—Ryan Yokota, fourth-generation Japanese American, reflecting on the pilgrimage to Manzanar concentration camp, April 1994

The experience of America's concentration camps is not just an event that affected a group of people a long time ago and then faded from memory. Rather, the camps had a lasting effect on all Americans, since the unconstitutional acts that allowed them to exist eroded every citizen's constitutional rights.

America's concentration camps have now become a collective experience. New knowledge is continually being uncovered. Old evidence is being reexamined. The lessons of the camps must not be forgotten. Remembering this event is a step toward preventing its repetition. To remember is to make America a better place for all its citizens.

Manzanar Pilgrimage, 1997. Photograph by Robert A. Nakamura.

Courage is something strong within you that brings out the best in a
person. Perhaps no one else may know or see, but it's those hidden
things unknown to others that reveal a person to God and self.
   —Yuri Nakahara Kochiyama


Despite the loneliness and despair that enveloped us, we made the
best we could with the situation. I hope when you look at these you
see the spirit of the people; people trying to reconstruct a community despite overwhelming obstacles. This, I feel, is the essence of
these home movies.
   —Dave Tatsuno


The words of Yuri Kochiyama, a political activist, and Dave Tatsuno,
one of the home movie makers featured, begin and end *Something Strong
Within,* the video production created for the exhibition. Directed by the
filmmaker Robert A. Nakamura, it consists solely of never-before-seen
home movies of camp life that we had discovered. If a picture is worth a
thousand words, moving pictures speak volumes, and these homemade
movies vividly expressed the inmates' dignity, humor, and tenacity like
no other medium could. We selected Kochiyama's and Tatsuno's statements because they symbolized the message of *Something Strong Within,*
which is that although the inmates had been done wrong, they were
not done in.
   *Something Strong Within* is not a typical documentary. There are no

interviews—no emotional commentary from inmates or analytical discourse by historians or sociologists. It does not even have a voice-over narration. Except for text cards that provide a brief summary of the incarceration at the beginning, quotations from inmates like Kochiyama and Tatsuno, and identification of sequences by home movie maker and camp, there is little didactic information presented in the film as the factual and historical context was provided by the exhibition itself. Instead, Nakamura created a multilayered piece using a palette of home movies that unfolded and played out to an evocative musical score with the express purpose of inviting the viewer to emotionally experience—rather than intellectually learn about—camp. The home movie genre poignantly captured the irony of living an American life—complete with football and baseball games, a preschool rhythm band, and high school baton twirlers—within the confines of American concentration camps equipped with barracks, barbed wire and guard towers. The music was scored and performed by Dan Kuramoto, leader of the jazz fusion band Hiroshima, and encouraged the audience to engage with these homemade images with their hearts rather than their heads.

The home movie makers featured and the camps documented included: Masayoshi Endo, Rohwer, Arkansas; Naokichi Hashizume, Heart Mountain, Wyoming; the brothers Akira and Yoshio Hayashi, Jerome and Rohwer, Arkansas; Norio Mitsuoka, Minidoka, Idaho; Eichi Sakauye, Heart Mountain, Wyoming; George Sahara, Amache, Colorado; Dave Tatsuno, Topaz, Utah; and Gunji Watanabe, Jerome and Rohwer, Arkansas. Franklin Johnson filmed the forced removal from Guadalupe, California. Rather than simply list these individuals in the end credits, we identified them throughout the production by name and camp when their footage appeared on the screen.

As the historian Robert Rosen writes later in this chapter, separate voices—those of the director, who had been incarcerated as a boy; the original home movie makers; and the composer, whose parents were in camp, all of whom are linked by the camp experience—converge to make *Something Strong Within* not merely a compilation piece but a work of art. In keeping with this multilayered approach, what follows are three pieces, from different points of view, that converge here to better

Identification of camp and home movie maker. From *Something Strong Within*. Original home movie footage taken by Norio Mitsuoka. JANM, 1994.

convey the message of *Something Strong Within*. The first is a conversation with Robert Nakamura, whose life and work have been greatly affected by his boyhood in camp. He explains that his two main goals for the film were to provide an experiential rather than academic understanding of camp and to get across the conviction that although victimized by their own government, the inmates were not simply victims. Next is an examination by the historian Robert Rosen of the historical memory embedded in the production. Rosen's analysis shows how the director's dual stance of restraint and advocacy combined to transform home movies beyond nostalgia into the realm of historical memory. As Rosen notes, it is only when viewers internalize a work that it becomes operative as a cultural force. Such a community perspective on the meaning of the film is offered by the third commentator in this chapter, the writer Joy Yamauchi. Yamauchi concludes, "The true power of this film lies in the fact that it does not apologize for showing scenes of children playing, people laughing and teasing. There is no apology needed."

## A Conversation with Robert A. Nakamura

Called the "godfather of Asian American media" for his pioneering work in the field, Robert A. Nakamura left a successful career in photojournalism and advertising photography to become one of the first to explore, interpret, and present the experiences of Japanese Americans on film, in the early 1970s.[1] His years in camp had a latent but long-term impact on his life and work. It was not just the years behind barbed wire that he had to reconcile. He had to come to grips with the aftershocks: having pledged allegiance to a country that betrayed his trust, needing to negotiate how to be American while having the face of the enemy, and being targeted by racism that assumes error and blame and then demands proof of innocence and worth. Nakamura explained:

> Camp has always been a theme in my work. I spent a little over two years of my childhood in Manzanar when I was five, six, and seven. Although I was pretty young at the time, it has played a central position in my life. Even at a young age I questioned why we

moved from our home to a barracks in the middle of the desert surrounded by barbed wire and armed guards. Yet for the most part I had a good time. There were lots of other kids around and we weren't made fun of or harassed by others for being who we were.

It was only later that I found out how much my folks lost, what havoc it wreaked on their emotional well being, how hard it was for them to rebuild our lives after the war. And then later to realize that only the Japanese—and not the Germans and Italians because they were white—were targeted, that there was no due process under law, that the Constitution could be so easily overridden, and on and on. When I learned about the injustice of it all, I felt guilty for having had a good time in camp, apologetic even. So camp has been fraught with ambivalence, a nostalgia mixed with deep resentment, and a lot of anger.[2]

Robert A. Nakamura is shown in the back row, sixth from the left, with his kindergarten class and their teacher in Manzanar. Courtesy of Robert A. Nakamura.

People deal with traumatic experiences in different ways. In the face of oppression there is always resistance, both political and spiritual. Artists confront the pain, invert it, and turn it into a force that drives them. They manifest this dynamic through many incarnations as they, and their relationship to it, change over time. As America's legacy of racism and discrimination has unleashed a lot of pain, it has unwittingly given rise to a lot of artistic expression, both raw and refined. Nakamura described how being in camp altered his awareness:

> Over time I've approached the experience in different ways in my films—in narrative format, documentary, docu-drama even—and I suppose I will continue to work it out. Emotionally, it was at camp that I lost my sense of innocence. From that time on I knew I would never grow up to be the president of the United States. Which means that before camp, I really thought I could.

With a B.F.A. from Art Center College of Design in Los Angeles, Nakamura developed a successful but ultimately unfulfilling career in advertising photography. He left to work as a photographer for the legendary designers Charles and Ray Eames and was inspired by their inventive and resourceful spirit of working and their creative projects and products. Still seeking his own way and buoyed by the emerging Asian American movement, Nakamura entered the M.F.A. program in film production at the University of California, Los Angeles.

His first film was *Manzanar* (1972, 8 mm, color, 16 minutes), a documentary on his recollections of being a child in camp. He approached the topic of camp from within, returning to the site for the first time since being released in 1945. In the process of creating the film, he began to recall incidents and feelings he thought were long forgotten. He began "interviewing" himself and recorded his responses into a tape recorder. Those recordings would become the film's voice-over narration. The result was groundbreaking. It was the first film on camp made by a former inmate. For almost thirty years it was, reportedly, the most utilized film on camp in classes and communities across the country. It was selected for retrospectives on the documentary form at the San Francisco Museum of Art and the Museum of Contemporary Art in Los

Angeles.[3] Most notably, it paved the way for subsequent films on camp and the Asian Pacific American experience. Nakamura has gone on to direct or executive produce ten other films and video productions in which camp has been the focal point. But it was *Manzanar,* his first film, that marked the unrepeatable moment when he turned his pain into power. Nakamura recalled:

> In *Manzanar,* for the first time, I went head-to-head with my feelings of being in camp. I didn't even know I remembered so much about camp until I did the film. There was so much ambivalence— between my childhood memories of having good times in camp and my outrage as an adult learning that it was so wrong. Going back the first time was really hard, but you know, like in the Castaneda books, Don Juan talks about finding your place of power? As weird as it may seem, I know that Manzanar is my place of power.

A shared experience, no matter how unjust the circumstances, creates an intimate and kindred universe for those who share it. Like it or not, camp became a defining moment for those who were there. Most of the surviving former inmates had been kids in camp. Like Nakamura, they spent precious childhood and teenage years behind barbed wire. During these formative years they were relatively untouched by what they learned later was an abrogation of their constitutional rights. Living communally in such close and unusual quarters, they spent more time with each other than they would have otherwise. Families lived in extremely close proximity to each other. Teenagers ate together in the mess hall instead of with their family units. Young adults met their spouses in camp. Thrown together within a barbed-wire compound and unable to get out, inmates formed bonds that transcended mere friendship and have endured collectively as well as individually through the years. This has led not only to lasting relationships but to camp reunions that have been held regularly since camp days and are well attended by people who often travel sizable distances.

This sentimentality attached to camp is puzzling to outsiders. When reflected in photographs, positive images of camp are found disturbing by outsiders. The camps look too nice; the inmates look too happy.

As Robert Rosen writes in this chapter, the behavior of camp residents as captured by home movies is in stark contradiction to the environment in which it takes place. Scenes of family and community solidarity are inextricably intertwined with images of desolate landscapes and the omnipresent barracks. People have a preconceived notion of what suffering or injustice should look like, and the inmates deviate from this. If the inmates are smiling, the judgment is that the camps must not have been so bad. The comparison with Nazi death camps further complicates the issue. Relative to death camps erected by a fascist dictatorship, America's concentration camps are not so bad. But because a democratic nation founded upon principles of freedom and liberty conceived and instituted the domestic camps, the very concept of American concentration camps is reprehensible.

Those whose experience this is do not see themselves as victims. This in itself can be confusing—exasperating even—as former inmates tend to emphasize the brighter side of the experience. As Nakamura said, memories of camp are fraught with ambivalence. To unravel this complexity, we need to remember that although the inmates were unwillingly incarcerated—and to that extent they were victims of the government's misuse of power—when physically confined they relied on their spirit. It was this spiritual stamina that enabled the inmates to "make the best of things." Nakamura said:

> The goal of *Something Strong Within* was to show the resistance that is inherent in making the best of things. It was not intended to be an educational film about camp as the exhibit would provide the historical context. It was meant to go beyond the facts and figures. I wanted to speak to ourselves—fellow inmates—who had been told it was for our own good, who were criminalized by the government we trusted while knowing we did nothing wrong, who were put in the position of being assumed guilty and having to prove our innocence instead of the other way around.

Regarding camp, Nisei often employ the phrase *shikataganai*. Literally translated, this means "it can't be helped," and from a Western viewpoint it is misunderstood as giving in. But from the Nisei's point of view it implies, "get over it," that is, make the best of it. And making the best of it meant smiling in the face of adversity, planting flowers in the desert, finding ways to have a good time in a concentration camp. Seemingly contradictory, acceptance is rarely seen as resistance; however, as the saying goes, living well is ultimately the best revenge. Nakamura said:

> Home movies were the key to why and how we approached *Something Strong Within* as we did. When I first saw these home movies that were taken by inmates in camp, they sent a chill up my spine. Nothing else had ever given me that visceral feel of being back in camp. By capturing the moment, the lens of the home movie maker provides that sense of being there, thereby allowing the viewer to experience camp rather than analyze it. This was the key to being able to show the spiritual resistance involved in making the best of things that I wanted to make known.

My work with home movies was on a more intellectual level than that of Nakamura. Convinced that the films constituted a unique cultural artifact, I was involved in legitimizing their value for preservation as well as championing their importance in the study of history and culture.[4] As part of this larger strategy to validate home movies, I advocated for their centralization in *Something Strong Within*—foregrounding them as documentary footage rather than regarding them as simply illustrative background information. I also wanted to acknowledge the home movie makers in the tradition of providing an artifact's provenance and to do so on screen, as one would treat excerpts from commercial films. Nakamura eventually reached the same conclusion. He said to me,

> Although we had done *Through Our Own Eyes*, when we first started I still thought this film [*Something Strong Within*] needed other elements. I shot a lot of artifacts and letters that were in the museum's collection and intended to include taped interviews of former inmates. Artistically I didn't think that home movies alone would be able to hold up from a cinematic viewpoint. But once I started to really get into the home movies, I agreed with you. I saw the home movies as art in themselves, the art of everyday life which is what I wanted to convey.[5]

When Nakamura was a student at Art Center College, he studied two types of photography: photojournalism, which is documentary in nature, capturing life as it happens, traditionally with a small, unobtrusive 35 mm camera; and its opposite, advertising photography, which uses premeditated and designed still-lifes with a large-format camera. He discovered that selection of photographic approach, type of camera, and film size influence the way viewers respond to the subject photographed. The photojournalistic approach, in its attempt to capture the decisive moment, is perceived as more authentic than advertising photography, and Nakamura applied that same approach in creating *Something Strong Within*. In editing, he went with—instead of against—the small-gauge format, maintaining the home movie's inconsistent focus and unsteady camera movements, and letting the sequences run long in order to provide the experiential sense of being there.

To further this visitor experience, we decided against using an omniscient narrator telling the viewers what they were seeing and instead substituted a carefully constructed musical score, composed and performed by Dan Kuramoto, to guide the viewer. Music was a critical element and considered the third component in a three-way artistic collaboration, which included Nakamura and myself, and the original home movie makers. Like Nakamura, Kuramoto was both a product and a shaper of the Asian American movement in the 1970s and 1980s that created a political and cultural revolution in our communities. A Sansei whose parents and grandparents were in camp, Kuramoto had long grappled with his own legacy of camp and therefore was able to infuse the music with a sensibility that enhanced rather than overpowered the integrity of the home movies.

Making *Something Strong Within* continued Nakamura's personal journey of coming to grips with camp. He immersed himself in each home movie collection, reviewing footage over and over again, eventually being able to recognize each person's shooting style. The home movies contained a level of verisimilitude that he had not encountered before. They captured the essence of camp life that still lay deep within him. He sought to enthrall the viewer in the same manner in which he found himself enthralled. He commented:

At this point in history, it's time to present ourselves to ourselves from our own point of view. Making *Something Strong Within* was very personal. I was tired of being cast as a victim, as totally powerless and needing a white protagonist to protect us, made to feel apologetic and grateful for a handout. People who went through camp don't see themselves as victims. They were consciously and deliberately trying to make the best out of a bad situation. This in itself is a form of resistance.

## Historical Memory and Something Strong Within
Robert Rosen

*Something Strong Within* poses a wide range of conceptual and theoretical questions of interest to anyone concerned with the use of moving image materials as historical narrative. What constitutes historical memory? How is it created and disseminated? Who makes it? Who consumes it; and to what uses is it put?[6]

But the subjective insistence of Nakamura's legacy of personal memories suggest questions of a different kind. How was camp life actually experienced by those who were there? What was the texture of daily life for ordinary people as viewed from the eye-level perspective of those who lived it? What insights are to be gained from an intensely subjective and nonjudgmental empathy with the seemingly mundane routines of day-to-day existence?

With these questions in mind, what resource could be more ideally suited for conveying the subjective realities of camp life than home movies shot by inmates in camp? Despite the alienating context of the camps, the cameramen (they were all men)—very much in the spirit of home movie makers—focused on subject matter that underscored the continuity of daily life.

In order to fully realize the potential of the home movies to capture life as it was lived, Nakamura made several key decisions in strategizing the film's construction. The first was to restrict all of the film's visual information solely to home movie footage. Another was to prominently foreground the identity of the men who shot the films. A third strategic decision was to maintain the essential integrity of their work by editing within collections and presenting the works in the spirit of their original conception instead of following the more familiar path of freely editing amateur film footage in conformity with the narrative intent of the filmmaker.

Most critically, based on the conviction that the images must speak for themselves, Nakamura adopted the risky and self-effacing strategy of directorial restraint. Explanatory and ideological framing devices are kept to a minimum. There is no contrived dialogue, no melodramatic musical score, no fancy editing, and no significant laboratory transformation of the footage. By allowing the home movies to stand on their own, and by maintaining a low directorial profile, Nakamura enhances the empathetic involvement of viewers with what is on the screen.

How did Nakamura, without appearing to have intervened at all, transform what could have been merely a compilation film into a fresh interpretive analysis? While presenting the home movies in the spirit they were originally conceived, beneath the surface Nakamura tightly structured a narrative in three acts preceded by a prologue and interrupted after the second act by an ironic interlude.

In the cinematic prologue before the opening titles, the story of life within the camps is prefaced by the only sequence depicting activities outside their boundaries and the sole footage shot by a home movie maker who was not himself a prisoner. Sensitively filmed by a Caucasian superintendent of schools in California, it shows Japanese American men, women, and children under military scrutiny being loaded onto buses for places unknown.

The prologue establishes the tangible reality of normal American life prior to the camps as a fixed reference point against which to gauge the severity of what follows. These compelling images depicting involuntary departure under armed guard remain with us for the entire film and serve as a subconscious corrective to any tendency to equate the significance of behavior in the context of a free community with ostensibly similar activities in a setting of involuntary incarceration.

Act 1 is unrelentingly grim. Nakamura selected the grainiest, darkest, and most abused footage to introduce the camps: barely visible images printed on badly scratched and deteriorating film stock. Overexposed ghostlike apparitions of isolated individuals are set against the surreal backdrop of desolate landscapes and makeshift streets. The images have the qualities we associate with troubling memories, remembrances so painful we desperately want to repress them, but so powerful that they force their way into consciousness. Like the prologue, the first act is intended to set an emotional tone that is an anticipatory corrective to possible misinterpretation of the images to follow.

Act 2 encompasses sequences shot at a number of camp locations by separate amateurs. The same types of activities and conditions—hostile weather, food preparation, dull camp architecture, and crowds of people eating together in huge communal mess halls—thematically reappear. Images that subjectively affirm the humanity of the people in the camp—acts of communal sharing, expressions of familial affection, evidences of artistic expression, or simply the presence of smiling faces—alternate with scenes that foreground the realities of hardship: incessant wind, intolerable weather conditions, guard towers, bleak barracks. The impact of this alternation on the spectator is not simply additive but dialectical. Each image inflects the other and thereby alters its meaning and emotional resonance. A simple expression of affection among family members reveals its deeper complexity when it is followed with images of a camp that, by its very existence, served to destabilize family life. Affirmations of humanity in such a dehumanizing setting becomes an implicit refusal to accept the grinding logic of long-term incarceration.

Following act 2 there is a brief ironic interlude. Suddenly, the contemplative musical score is interrupted by the strident tones of a Boy Scout drum-and-bugle corps, the only actual sounds in the film recorded in the camps. Sgt. Ben Kuroki, a celebrated Army Air Corps tail gunner—and also a Japanese American—is triumphantly welcomed as a war hero to the camp that is prison to other Japanese Americans. Adding to the understated irony of this commentary is footage of a gala parade, complete with American flags fluttering in the breeze, military music, festooned grandstand, and Kuroki shaking hands with a fellow soldier—but one who is Caucasian and guarding the camp.

Act 3 returns to the undulating rhythms of act 2, but as the narrative moves toward its conclusion the tonal contradictions grow increasingly

Exclusion of Japanese Americans from Guadalupe, California, by U.S. Army. From the opening sequence of *Something Strong Within*. Original home movie footage taken by Franklin Johnson. Courtesy Grace Nakamura. JANM, 1994.

Welcoming Sgt. Ben Kuroki in Heart Mountain. From *Something Strong Within.* Original home movie footage taken Edward Eiichi Sakauye. JANM, 1994.

intense. On the one side there are some of the film's most inspiring images: children graduating from grammar school and a community art class taught by a distinguished painter. On the other side we see the natural elements at their worst, as if they were attacking the camp with wind, snow, and blistering sun. The technical quality of the images are among the best and the musical score hints at the possibilities for drawing positive lessons from what has been shown.

The concluding scene carries with it the filmmaker's core message about life in the camps without his ever having to deliver it directly. A solitary teen-age girl skates awkwardly on a frozen pond, or more accurately a large manmade puddle, behind a black tar-paper-covered barrack. We see at once: the girl's determination to wrest the joys customarily associated with growing up from seemingly impossible circumstances; the improvised skating rink, no doubt the result of communal effort; the camp's lifeless architecture, a reminder of its function as place of confinement; and the existential loneliness that results from being forced to live outside the boundaries of a free society. When taken as a whole, these elements come together to transform commonplace recreational activity into a powerful expression of refusal—the unwillingness of an individual and her community—to accept the diminished status of prisoners without hope.

From the perspective of film as an expression of historical memory, although they played no role at all in the film's creation it is only when viewers internalize a work that it becomes operative as a cultural force. At one extreme, there are historical films that strive to seduce a spectator into becoming a passive recipient of the film's point of view through the use of manipulative rhetorical and stylistic devices to drive home a predetermined message. *Something Strong Within* finds a way to present as persuasively as possible the filmmakers' interpretive approach while at the same time encouraging an autonomous and self-directed spectator.

To achieve these seemingly contradictory goals simultaneously, the film relies primarily on two textual strategies that recur in various forms throughout the work. The first divides spectator attention among a multiplicity of perspectives, thereby problematizing the narrative, discouraging passive viewing, and encouraging interaction with the work.

The second persistently foregrounds unresolvable cognitive oppositions that evoke disquieting feelings of emotional dissonance. The quest for relief leads spectators to dig more deeply into the underlying meaning of what is presented on the screen.

In *Something Strong Within*, the coexistence of multiple "voices" that retain their integrity as separate points of view is expressed. Instead of becoming suppliers of stock footage, the picture takers retain their identity and are elevated to the status of players within the historical narrative itself and co-creators of the film's overall meaning. At the same time, without negating the autonomy of the picture takers, the director's point of view is conveyed by his sequencing of the home movies to arrive at an implicit narrative and by his discreet use of interpretive framing devices. While the musical score supports the director's narrative, it has a voice of its own and never simply duplicates the emotional content of specific images. The music's contemplative pacing and subtle tonalities invite spectators to seek broader meaning from what they see. Finally, through their behavior and demeanor, the people in the camps are also allowed to retain their own voice, free from the distortions that might have resulted from manipulative editing, voice-over narration, or melodramatic scoring.

At the same time that multiple voices augment spectator empathy, they also promote the emotional distancing necessary for intellectual reflection. An interplay of independent perspectives suggests to spectators that the ultimate significance of the events depicted on screen remains an unresolved question that calls for their participation. An implicit open-ended dialogue among the picture takers, filmmakers, and people in the camps encourages viewers to add their own voices to the discussion.

The second narrative strategy that runs throughout the film is the presentation of unresolved and possibly irresolvable oppositions that leave spectators with an unsettling feeling of dissonance. Elements are juxtaposed that cannot be reconciled with one another emotionally, intellectually, or cognitively. For example, positive and negative commentary are indissolubly fused in two scenes dealing with Japanese American soldiers—one showing a group of GIs being entertained at a USO situated inside the camp, the other a gala welcome-"home" celebration for a local war hero. Simultaneously the images affirm the patriotic loyalties of Japanese Americans and subversively undercut that very same affirmation by questioning the rationality of patriotism in the context of a prison camp.

There is also a degree of spectator dissonance at a metatextual level resulting from a clash of expectations ordinarily associated with home movies and historical documentaries. Home movies convey the immediacy of personal experience and are assumed to be of interest only within the sphere of the family and immediate intimates. Historical documentaries attempt to draw more overarching conclusions and speak to a broader and more anonymous audience. Home movies are usually overwhelmingly positive in what they show; historical documentaries show the realities of the past, whatever they may be. Thus, there is something unnerving about seeing a supposedly naive film form transformed into a devastatingly powerful document recording one of the grimmest episodes in the history of American civil liberties. When cognitively incompatible communications are combined with the undeniable facticity of photographic images, the result is a troubling discordance that cries out for resolution. In so far as the answers cannot be found by relying on a reading of surface content alone, and in the absence of didactic framing by the filmmaker, there is a powerful incentive for spectators to dig more deeply into the work and to mobilize their own analytical and intuitive resources.

It is difficult to avoid arriving at the conclusion that, above all else, the Japanese American community survived the dehumanizing and destabilizing impact of long-term confinement by drawing on a profoundly unshakable inner strength. They exhibited an unabiding and dogged determination to lead normal lives in abnormal circumstances and thereby resist both personal and cultural disintegration. The quiet dignity of ordinary people leading ordinary lives is, in the end, a form of resistance. They resisted the inclination to lose hope in the face of daunting challenges, to abandon the future of their children, to deny a cultural identity and community solidarity that had singled them out for persecution in the first place, and, most surprising of all, to abandon their commitment to a nation that had abandoned them.

## No Apology Needed: A Community Perspective
Joy Yamauchi

Indulge me a bit. *Something Strong Within: Home Movies from America's Concentration Camps* is shown continuously at the Japanese American National Museum's exhibit, "America's Concentration Camps." If you haven't seen it, you must and then you must see it again and again. Like peeling an onion, each viewing reveals layers and layers of new insights.[7]

"Courage is something strong within you that brings out the best in a person. Perhaps no one else may know or see, but it's those hidden things unknown to others that reveals a person to God and self." Yuri Nakahara Kochiyama wrote those words in her diary on May 3, 1942. Kochiyama is a woman known for her personal courage and strength, but these home movies are a testimony to the strength of the people who survived the internment and did so with great dignity.

Told without compromise (and without narration) the film opens with a street scene in Guadalupe, California. Taken by the school principal, Japanese Americans are seen getting on busses headed for camp. A lone hand raises a silent farewell.

From there, the film captures all aspects of camp life: a girl runs through the high winds trying to outrace the oncoming dust storm; a baby cries soundlessly and is comforted by an adult; women make paper flowers for a funeral wreath; people trudge though the snow, their breath frozen plumes caught on film and frozen forever.

Each time I saw the film, I heard people around me murmuring quietly, "Oh yes, that's what it was like." "Remember how cold it was?" "Remember the dust?" "The mess hall—sometimes they gave us three starches for dinner, rice, potatoes and pasta." "A baseball game, everybody came out when there was a baseball game. Well, there was nothing else to do. Any diversion brought a crowd." "The lines, we lined up for everything. Remember getting sick and having to line up for the latrine?" "That powdered soap in the laundry room, I used to wash my hair with that."

Parts of the film have a surprisingly contemporary look. A few clips are in color, one showing young men in plaid flannel shirts and blue jeans cutting wood, laughing with easy good humor. It could be almost any contemporary setting. Then you see the young skirted women, splitting wood, their bare hands heaving those heavy axes.

There is such beauty and power in this film. There are women, doing laundry by hand with steam rising around them, laughing and talking as they work the washboard. In another scene, children solemnly practice dancing for *obon*, their faces serious in concentration. Men are filmed *sumo* wrestling, the dust rises as their bare bottoms hit the earth. In a Christmas clip, a badly made up Santa Claus hands a child a gift with forced gaiety. A young man joyously dances with reckless abandon. The images are mesmerizing.

It would be so simple to look at this film and say, "There, look. They're enjoying themselves. They're playing baseball, running races, holding parades, dancing, having fun. They don't look like they are suffering at all."

Truth is, there are no scripted scenes of misery, no one caught sobbing in uncontrolled grief. These are home movies. Yet unlike home movies taken under normal circumstances, there is an underlying poignancy that transcends the innocent, naive faces on the screen. In one scene, a solitary girl ice skates slowly, the camera following her feet as she circles the frozen ice. In another, a girl brushes her hair before a small mirror, seemingly unaware of the camera behind her. Throughout the film, the wind is heard in the background. The message is clear—life continues, people endure, they survive.

In 1943, Taro Suma wrote, "On the first day at the mess hall I came upon the true meaning of life. At the bottom of my darkness I saw the reflection of my wife and children."

Watching the film opens up so many questions about the stories left untold. At a recent slide show on the internment, I found myself thinking of all the toddlers who underwent toilet training when the latrines were so far away. A woman told me about a young family traveling to camp—the two small children had the measles and the parents had no-where to lay them down on the train, so the parents and children sat up the entire way. The children probably infected the entire train along the way. Listening to the comments about eating three starches for dinner, you think about what kind of prenatal care pregnant women had and the pain of childbirth in such a desolate situation. Watching the women make paper flowers for a funeral wreath, you wonder who comforted the dying and what those last days must have been like.

The true power of this film lies in the fact that it does not apologize for showing scenes of children playing, people laughing and teasing. There is no apology needed. These people made the most of the situation. That they were able to reconstruct a community (or some semblance to one) in these overwhelming circumstances, is a true testimony to their courage.

And in watching this film, I am in awe of that strength, and of their beauty.

● ● ●

In the end, like all films, *Something Strong Within* is a mediated experience, a collaborative artistic endeavor to show what the title states forthright. Situated as it was within an historical exhibition on camp, it sought not to recapitulate the facts and figures but to maximize the home movie's ability to bring the viewer into the moment and convey a deeper understanding. It was also part of a larger strategy to promote the significance of this small-gauge, consumer format within the realm of its own medium. Despite these curatorial agendas, *Something Strong Within* took on a life of its own outside the exhibition and the realm of home movies. It garnered six awards including a CINE Golden Eagle, first place in the history category and second best of all categories from the American Association of Museums. It was selected for twelve film festivals including the Yamagata International Documentary Film Festival in Japan and the Robert Flaherty Seminar for Independent Film and Cinema in New York. While discussed here in print, it's greater distinction lies in the showing rather than the telling.

# 6 / Los Japoneses Que Hablan Español and Other Stories That Walked in the Door

On the opening day of the exhibition, an elderly Mexican American man and a young, long-haired Chicano man mingled amidst the crowd of primarily Japanese Americans and their families. The elder clutched something in a paper bag to his chest as he carefully viewed the photographs, read the text panels, and looked at the artifacts. The younger man followed his lead. Approaching a staff member, the elder took out a worn 1941 high school yearbook from the paper bag. The young man explained that his grandfather had gone to high school in the area and had many Japanese American friends. The grandfather opened up the yearbook to show a few pages of young, eager youths in senior portraits—a common icon of American teenage hood—and ran his finger mindfully across the faces of the Japanese American youth. The grandson said that one day all his grandfather's Japanese American friends seemed to have disappeared and he didn't know why. "My grandfather says he just wanted someone to know that they were his good friends and that he still remembers them."

Throughout the exhibition there were stories like these that literally walked in the door. On the opening weekend a record number of over six thousand visitors attended the exhibition. By the end of its eleven-month run we were gratified to find out that 50 percent of the seventy thousand visitors were other than Japanese Americans. While we had always thought of the mass exclusion and incarceration as an American story and not an exclusively Japanese American concern, visitors of various ethnicities confirmed the fact that it had indeed been part of many personal and public histories in strange, often unsettling, and even wonderful ways.

## The Man Who Used to Be White

It was Sunday evening, the end of the opening weekend of the exhibition. Jean Hamamoto, a longtime volunteer, called me to say there was a Caucasian man in the lobby and although she couldn't understand everything he said, he seemed to have an interesting story and wanted to talk to someone about the exhibition. Would I be able to come down?

He was a middle-aged man—fifty-three, I soon learned—and seemed very nervous and uneasy. He carried a small latched container that he fiddled with as we sat in the lobby, the remaining staff and volunteers taking their leave around us. He spoke haltingly and his words spurted out unevenly: his mother had died, he didn't know whether he should have come here or not, there was a locked box, even his cousins had no idea, he heard about the exhibition on the radio and drove two hours to get here, he finally found a ring of keys but which one was it? I listened hard trying to assess whether this man was a little off or, after the many hard months of working on the exhibition, it was I who had finally exceeded my physical and mental capacity. He kept referring to "this person." I kept listening. Little by little his story unfolded.

His mother had died years ago and he had put her belongings away, intending to go through them later. As time allowed, he sorted through her things, keeping some, tossing others. Each time, he noticed among her possessions a box that was locked. But there were so many items that he had to deal with, so many other boxes that could be opened, that the locked box was overlooked until the next time he found time to continue his task. One time, he found a ring with many keys. Another time, he had a moment and just for the heck of it decided to try each key in the lock, key after key—until one did the trick and the box opened.

He kept talking to me, his speech and delivery now steadied as he concentrated on the container with which he had been fidgeting. Slowly he opened the box and gingerly brought out its contents. There were some old papers that appeared to be documents and letters. I waited for him to unfold them and show them to me. He brought out two small portraits that looked like they were from the early 1920s—one of a Caucasian woman in a white high-collared blouse and the other of an Issei man in work clothes. Some of the papers were clearly War Relocation Authority documents and apparently belonged to the man in the photo. His camp address was marked on one. He was identified as a single male with no family.

When my visitor first opened the container a few years earlier, he wasn't prepared for what turned out to be a Pandora's box. In the task-oriented mode of sorting and tossing, he was ready to do the same when he came upon these things. He was shocked and alarmed. What was a picture of this "Oriental" man doing amongst his mother's things? Why had it been locked away? Who was this person? What was a "relocation center"? And always back to the question, What had these things to do with his mother and hence with him?

It had been two years since he first opened the box. He talked with his brothers, sisters, and cousins and they were as alarmed as he was. Eventually he made the staggering discovery that the Caucasian woman in the high lace collar was his mother's mother and that the Japanese man in the photograph was his grandfather. His grandfather had been Japanese. This newfound knowledge shook the very foundation of this white, middle-aged, and admittedly conservative man and rendered everything that was built on it—his values, his thoughts, his actions, his identity—insecure and unstable.

While still uncertain of some of the details, he found out that they had married in the 1920s, when interracial marriages were not only uncommon but also illegal. Apparently, because of the intensity of discrimination and intolerance, his mother and her siblings assumed their mother's maiden name and went through college and adulthood—and eventually into marriages and families of their own—evidently passing for white. During the forced exclusion and mass incarceration, his grandfather maintained he was single, presumably to protect his family, and went to camp alone. Reportedly, family members kept up some contact with him by writing and sending him things, never revealing their true relationship. My visitor never found out what became of his grandfather after the war.

By this time, the man was focused, intense, and close to tears, as was I. He said when he heard about the exhibition, he impulsively got in his car with his Pandora's box and drove two hours to the museum. By the time he arrived, he wondered if he should have come. Was the museum just for Japanese Americans? Would we deride and reject him for his connection? I assured him the museum was for everyone and that his story was not only welcome but was one of the many little-known episodes that help us better understand this American story. He looked me straight in the eye and admitted that, growing up a white male, he had his prejudices. He didn't elaborate; he didn't need to. Caustically he said, "Here I am this white guy—or I used to be."

It was clear that this was a man with a heavy heart. He spoke his thoughts out loud. He tried to recall his mother's life for any signs of her hidden secret. She didn't look anything but white; neither had his uncles and aunts. But, he recalled, she seemed to have a lot of sympathy for the survivors of the Hiroshima and Nagasaki atomic bombs. Looking back on it, was that because she herself was half Japanese? Why had she never told him? He was filled with anguish, not only for himself but also in empathy for this Japanese grandfather he never knew. How painful it must have been to live amidst so much discrimination. How difficult a decision to deny his family for their safety. How lonely.

I told him about the camp registry and how descendants of inmates who have passed on are invited to remember them and leave their mark by entering their name. Although the exhibition was closed, I asked if he would like to see it and sign the registry for himself and his grandfather. We went upstairs; I turned the lights on in the gallery and oriented him to the exhibition. Taking in all the photos, the camp layouts, and the display cases filled with artifacts, he seemed in awe of the reality and enormity of the event he had only recently learned about. We discovered that someone from the same barracks his grandfather had been in had signed the registry. While this meant that his barracks had already been placed on the map, it also signified that these people might actually have known his grandfather, the thought of which was very dear. He signed his grandfather's name, retrieving him from among the nameless and in this case the forgotten, and reclaimed his part in history. I wished that I had access to the Polaroid camera to add his picture to the camp album, but it was locked up in the volunteers' office.

He seemed genuinely moved that he could acknowledge his grandfather in this way. This was one of the few things he could actually do with the discovery that had altered his identity. I invited him to come back whenever he liked. He said he had a lot more of his grandfather's things and a lot more questions. I said I was very interested in seeing them and learning more about their story. He promised to return but never has. I've thought of him many times since. He gave me his phone number and I have often thought of calling him. But Pandora's boxes, although bewitching on the outside, can be ominous when opened. I had become witness to a secret that had been held for three generations. As genuine a moment it had been at the time—for him to share it and for me to hear it—there are reasons we tell strangers our secrets; it's because they are strangers.

## Classified Caucasians

Rev. Kitagawa's words appeared in the exhibition under the headline "Life behind Barbed Wire."[1] The panel on which it appeared displayed photographs and quotations intended to provide an impressionistic feel for the variety and complex characterizations of life in camp. The notion that "even Negroes were classified as Caucasians" seems ridiculous, but so is racism. Rha and Kimberly Nickerson brought their story to the museum, corroborating this fact and adding to the mounting evidence that this was truly an American story that had crossed color lines.

Their mother was Rhetta Jean Mitchell, now deceased, who had been the chief dietitian at the Central Utah Relocation Center, commonly known as Topaz.

> The center was a place where Caucasian people governed and Japanese people were governed. The official policy was to discourage fraternization between colonists and appointed personnel, all of whom were Caucasian Americans; for administrative purposes even Negroes were classified as Caucasians.
>
> —The Reverend Daisuke Kitagawa

Originally from Los Angeles, Rhetta Jean was a graduate of Wilberforce University in Ohio, had completed her internship in St. Louis, and was working in Chicago before being recruited to go to Topaz. When she first arrived in July 1944, life in America was still very much segregated. Mitchell was relieved and ecstatic to meet another African American woman, Lieutenant Emma Perkins, USNC, who was a nurse at the Topaz Hospital. Perkins had also been a nurse at the Tule Lake camp in California. The two women learned to call each other *obasan*, the Japanese word for "aunt," and formed a lifelong friendship.

Rha and Kimberly, entranced by the stories their mother told them—of working in an American concentration camp, of making Japanese American friends and learning some Japanese, of her special friendship with Emma Perkins—were eager to meet anyone who might have known their mother in camp. They contacted the Topaz reunion committee. They found Perkins living in Washington, D.C., and offered to bring her out for the reunion. Emma was reportedly delighted but had to decline at the last minute because of health concerns. Rha and Kimberly conducted a telephone interview with her on November 10, 1990:

Rha: What years were you at these different concentration camps?

Emma: I was there from 1944 till '46. I was at Tule Lake one year, in California. And I was at Topaz, Arizona, two years. And you want me to tell you? When your mother came, the train stopped in Topaz, Utah, in the middle of the night. The Japanese operated in the early morning, after midnight, because of the humidity and the heat. The daytime was too hot, and they didn't have access to the air conditioning that they have now. So the Japanese would get up at midnight and set up and operate for the next day.

Rha: Okay, so Mama came in, in the middle of the night, because of the medical staff's schedule?

Emma: Well, we assumed that she came because of the secrecy. The Caucasians didn't accept Negroes hardly better than they did the Japanese. And so her being a Negro, she came in on the midnight train. I was in the operating room. And the superintendent came and said, "It's a Miss Mitchell"—she was Mitchell then—"a dietitian

**ON LEAVE**—Chief Dietitian Rhetta Jean Mitchell and Lieut. Emmie W. Perkins, USNC, Topaz, Utah, War Relocation Camp Hospital Aides, recently enjoyed a fortnight's leave in Los Angeles following a year and a half's service at the Japanese-American relocation center. Lieutenant Perkins hails from Chicago, and Mrs. Mitchell, wife of Capt. Joe Mitchell, 268th Station Hospital in the Philippines, is from Los Angeles.—Cutler Photo.

## Served Nisei

# WRA Workers Visit Los Angeles

LOS ANGELES—Thoroughly enjoying themselves in Los Angeles during their fortnight's vacation stay, Lieut. Emmie W. Perkins, USNC, and Rhetta Jean Mitchell, chief dietitian, Topaz, Utah, Relocation Hospital, entrained Saturday en route to their post.

Both have been stationed at the Topaz Hospital for the past year and a half. Previously, Lieutenant Perkins served at Tule Lake, Oregon. She was there when riots broke out and several persons were killed and injured.

**CALLED "CAUCASIANS"**

Lieutenant Perkins and Mrs. Mitchell are the only two persons of their race employed at the center. Along with the several hundred other male and female employees they are called "caucasians" by the Japanese.

Both indicated they might seek future employment at Sawtelle Soldiers Home in Los Angeles or one of several Army hospitals in Southern California.

**HUSBAND IN PACIFIC**

Mrs. Mitchell is a native of Los Angeles, and is a graduate of Wilberforce University. She interned at Homer G. Phillips Hospital in St. Louis, and served on the staff at Provident Hospital in Chicago. Her parents are Mr. and Mrs. William Boswell. Her husband is Capt. Joe Mitchell of Houston, presently serving in the Philippines.

Lieutenant Perkins is from Chicago and graduated from the Chicago School of Nursing. She also worked at Provident and has been in Government Relocation service for the past three years.

Newspaper article about Rhetta Jean Mitchell and Emma Perkins in Topaz. Collection of JANM, gift of the Nickerson Family (97.51.1).

is here." And when I saw her, she was frightened to death, standing behind the door. And we saw each other; we caressed and jumped up and down. And that was the beginning of a beautiful friendship that lasted forever.

Rha: Now, you were probably there about a year before she came in. Had there been other . . .

Emma: Negroes? No. No, we were the only two Negroes—I don't mind being called a Negro—we were the only two Negroes there, but we were called "Caucasian." We were classified as Caucasian by the staff, that meant the Caucasian staff, and whenever they referred to us, we were referred to as Caucasian.

Rha: Now is this the government's classification?

Emma: Yes, this is the government's classification. They never called us Negro.

Rha: Isn't that something.

Emma: But that's the truth. Yes, we were classified under the count of the Caucasian, and referred to as Caucasian. And they did some mixed-up stuff, but we were Caucasian at that length of time. . . . The attitude of the Caucasian towards the Orientals was very arrogant and hostile, and unfair and unkind. And you can quote me as saying that. I don't mind, because I am telling the truth. I don't mind.[2]

## The Japanese Ghosts in the BIA Boarding School

In March 1995, Jane Lockard and Mary Ann Goodluck from the Chinle Primary School Literacy Center in Arizona were attending an English as a Second Language (ESL) meeting in Los Angeles and were advised to visit America's Concentration Camps. I happened to meet them in the exhibition hall. As we talked, Lockard told me that her young nephews Ben and Ken Lockard and their friend Melvin Nez had produced a video on the Japanese American incarceration for a History Day project at Flagstaff High School. They focused on the Leupp Isolation Center in Arizona, the little-known prison camp run by the War Relocation Authority (WRA), which had been located on Navajo land. "A prison within a prison," quipped Goodluck, herself a Navajo.

In addition to the ten concentration camps, the WRA established two isolation camps to separate so-called troublemakers from people in the other camps. However, accusations of their "crimes," such as instigating work stoppages and making "disloyal" statements, were made in a capricious and arbitrary manner. Flagrant mistakes were made and innocent persons seized.[3]

The first isolation center was established on the site of a Civilian Conservation Corps camp at Moab, Utah, on December 10, 1942. In April 1943 it was moved to Leupp, Arizona. In Leupp, eighty inmates were guarded by one hundred fifty military police. Francis S. Frederick, the chief of internal security at Moab and Leupp, conceded, "How in hell can you Americanize the Japs when Gestapo methods are used in sending them to Leupp—no warrants, no trials, no sentence, separated from their families, etc."[4] The site closed on December 2, 1943, and the remaining prisoners were transferred to the Tule Lake Segregation Center in California.

Jane Lockard felt there were a lot of similarities between the ways Japanese Americans and Indians were treated. Certainly, over a hundred years before Japanese Americans were uprooted and forced from their homes, tens of thousands of Choctaw, Chickasaw, Creek, Cherokee, and Seminole peoples from the southeast were forced to move westward along the "Trail of Tears" in an attempt to make the New World literally a white man's country. Many WRA camps had been constructed on American Indian land. Gila River was built on the reservation of the Gila River Indian community in Arizona. Heart Mountain in Wyoming and Minidoka in Idaho were also on Indian land. Poston, on Indian land in Arizona, was even first administered by the Bureau of Indian Affairs (BIA).

Lockard said that a large number of WRA staff came from the BIA, which was already seasoned in the bureaucracy of colonization. The BIA-WRA connection was maintained after the war by Dillon S. Myer. Myer was director of the WRA from 1942 until its closing in 1946 and became director of the BIA in 1950. In his biography of Myer, Richard Drinnon points out similarities between the way the U.S. government handled American Indians and the methods it used with Japanese

Americans. He quotes Francis Frederick's assessment of the Gila police chief: "Indian Service for ten years and like all of those guys feels that there are only two kinds of Indians—gooduns and baduns—and feels that Japs are Indians."[5] The indoctrination to "civilize" the Indians was used also to "Americanize" the Japanese Americans. Japanese American inmates in Poston reportedly asked "if they would be 'kept' the rest of their lives on reservations like Indians."[6]

Jane Lockard brought a copy of the Lockard brothers' and Melvin Nez's ambitious and well-chosen video project, which we viewed in my office. The three had found and interviewed Harry Ueno, who had been active in trying to organize kitchen workers at Manzanar and was subsequently arrested and shipped first to Moab and then to Leupp. They interviewed eighty-year-old Lucion Long, a Navajo employed as a guard at the Leupp Isolation Center. Although he spoke English, he indicated that because he wanted his testimony to be correct, he would speak in his own language. Melvin's father, Melvin Nez Sr., provided voice-over translation of Long's interview. The sight and sound of this Navajo elder speaking in Navajo about the Japanese American incarceration strikingly illustrated that this event was not just a Japanese American story. Justin White, a Navajo teacher who grew up in and near Leupp, stated in the film that there had been a lot of resentment against the Japanese American prisoners at the time, partly because of the intrusion on the American Indians' land and partly because so many American Indians fought and lost their lives in World War II. This too reflected the complexity and irony of the situation. The hapless prisoners were Americans citizens who had been uprooted and incarcerated without due process and then imprisoned for supposed crimes on other Americans' land without permission or protocol. In addition, although they were Americans, they looked like the enemy.

Adding to the irony, the site of the isolation center that held Japanese Americans during the war was the location of a dreaded BIA boarding school for Navajos both before and after the war, making Leupp a place of confinement for two of America's dislocated minorities over the years. Lockard said that people who had been sent to the boarding school after the war remembered that they had been told not to go into certain parts of the school because "Japanese ghosts lived there." Unrecorded in the official records, the shared history of Leupp, Arizona, filters into popular memory as mythology.

## Los Japoneses Que Hablan Español

In conjunction with the exhibition, the National Museum organized public programs under the direction of Alison Kochiyama. Public programs were a way to provide greater insight into various aspects of the incarceration, foster dialogue and discussion with the general public, and encourage people to explore issues more deeply. Through them, Kochiyama and I attempted to make known how other ethnic groups were part of the camp story. The history of Crystal City illustrated this intersection and in the end demonstrated how Chicanos and Japanese Americans turned this place of injustice into a place of empowerment.

As previously described, Crystal City was unusual in many ways. It was the only family camp in the Justice Department's internment system, built to house families who opted to join their husbands and fathers who had been arrested after Pearl Harbor. While originally intended to detain only Japanese, it interned over 1,000 Germans and one Italian family who were released following Italy's surrender.[7] Crystal City also had the dubious distinction of interning most of the more than 2,260 Japanese Latin Americans who were forcibly deported from thirteen Latin American countries in an ill-conceived and never-realized plot to exchange them for Americans held in Japan. On the closing of Crystal City, the Department of Justice Immigration and Naturalization Service claimed, "Except for the floodlighted ten-foot wire fence that surrounded the facility, the Crystal City Camp resembled any thriving and bustling southwestern town."[8]

Like Leupp, Crystal City had been a center of segregation and confinement for two different American minorities and was thrice anointed: as a migrant labor camp for Mexicans before the war, a concentration camp for Japanese Americans during the war, and a segregated school for migrant Mexican children after the war.

On February 25, 1995, we had the pleasure of bringing Alan Taniguchi and Dr. Jose Angel Gutierrez to the museum to talk about Crystal City's startling bicultural history. Taniguchi, whose family was incarcerated in Crystal City during World War II, was an award-winning architect and designed the memorial erected at the historic Crystal City site. Gutierrez, a well-known Chicano activist and attorney,[9] had attended the segregated school at the site as a boy. According to Taniguchi, Gutierrez was the first person to suggest that a memorial commemorating the incarceration of Japanese American be placed at Crystal City. The irony of the site and its uses were not lost on either man.

Alan Taniguchi's father, Isamu Taniguchi, was one of the "enemy aliens" interned at Crystal City. Alan, his mother, and younger brother, Izumi (who was my uncle), were sent to Gila River in Arizona. His mother and brother moved to Crystal City to be reunited with his father while Alan got clearance to relocate to Detroit. Little did he know at the time that they would all eventually return to make Texas their home and he would become a key figure in turning this place of oppression into a site of reclamation.

Alan's father, who had once been designated an "enemy alien," would become "everybody's pal in Austin," according to the *San Antonio Express News* in 1985.[10] Deeply troubled by the bombing of Hiroshima and Nagasaki, the elder Taniguchi began making a Japanese garden with his own resources and dedicated it to world peace for the people of Austin, his adopted home. On its completion, the garden became a local treasure and favorite site for school field trips. A frequent speaker at local schools, Taniguchi would explain the necessity for world peace and ask each student to do their part by laying aside any anger and ill thoughts before entering the garden.

Alan became an architect and moved to Texas in 1952. He became knowledgeable about the state's Mexican American presence and influence and said, "I was able to relate to the plight of being a minority and found myself in a mutually simpatico relationship with the Mexican American communities. I found myself 100 percent politically aligned with the Latinos." He went on to become professor and dean of the School of Architecture at the University of Texas at Austin and was instrumental in establishing the Minority Scholarship Program of the American Institute of Architects (AIA).

Gutierrez was born and raised in *Cristal*. One of his first recollections was of hearing the elders of the area refer to a time when *los japoneses que hablan español* lived there. At the time he said he didn't think too much of it. Since he never knew any Japanese to live in the area, much less Japanese who spoke Spanish, he wrote it off in his young mind as just something old people talked about. Only much later did he realize that these elders were recalling the Japanese Latin Americans who had been deported from their country and incarcerated in Crystal City. After his father died, Gutierrez became a migrant worker along with his mother. In the 1950s he was sent to the segregated school for migrant children—on the site of the Crystal City Internment Camp. "Migrant," he said, was just another word for Mexican.

Gutierrez went on to obtain a Ph.D. and a law degree. In 1969, he was one of the founders of the La Raza Unida Party, which challenged the traditional political hierarchy and won seats on school boards, city councils, and county governments throughout Texas and California.[11] He was elected to the Crystal City Independent School District Board of Trustees and became the first Chicano to serve as board president. When he spoke at the museum, he was director of the Center for Mexican American Studies at the University of Texas at Arlington.

During Gutierrez's first year as president of the Crystal City school board, the subject of the Japanese American concentration camp came up many times. School supplies, desks, and books were stored in camp barracks. The local elementary school was in the former administration buildings, which still contained boxes of Japanese American student records from the internment days. A barracks was used to house bachelor teachers until housing could be found. The "whites only" Crystal City Country Club used two camp barracks as its clubhouse and social center.

That same year, the school board made plans to tear down the old structures, so resonant of its disgraceful past, and rebuild new, air-conditioned schools. Crystal City's urban renewal director was a former student of Taniguchi. When he told the school board about Taniguchi, a noted architect whose family had been incarcerated at Crystal City, the board hired Taniguchi to design the new schools. Gutierrez said, "The site with its horrible buildings had been hell holes for many of us Japanese Americans and Mexican Americans all these years. Personally I also wanted to have him bring his father back to *Cristal* to help us torch the place."

While they didn't "torch the place," they tore down the old structures that symbolized decades of oppression and erected new schools. But the story of reclamation and resistance did not end there. Gutierrez tried to have the campsite designated a national historic site and then a state historic site, but without success. He even contacted the Japanese government for support to build a replica of the camp and then the Mexican government about building a monument to both peoples. Taniguchi and his brother, my uncle Izumi, who was an active member of the Japanese American Citizens League and of the Crystal City Association, an organization of former internees, were approached by the superintendent of the Crystal City School District. Alan designed the memorial, and with Izumi's assistance, the Crystal City Association raised the necessary funds. In November 1985 the memorial was dedicated.

And so after decades, this former site of discrimination for both Mexican Americans and Japanese Americans was finally exorcised. Through the efforts of Alan Taniguchi and Jose Angel Gutierrez, the determination of both ethnic groups who shared the site, and the spirits of *los japoneses que hablan español,* the small town of Crystal City has a long and, in the end, victorious history.

• • •

These are a few of the stories that walked in the door of the museum during the run of America's Concentration Camps. Too often, as racial tensions continue to stalk this country, ethnic groups feel increasingly polarized. Yet people of color in the United States have always shared a common history simply by being nonwhite. In the exhibition, a text panel reminded visitors that the camps were not a result of the bombing of Pearl Harbor but in fact had their roots in the legacy of racism that has permeated the U.S. since its beginning. Throughout the course of the exhibition, stories such as these illustrated that while we maintain rich ethnic and cultural identities, our histories—and thus our futures—are intertwined.

At a public program called "Coming to Terms: The Impact of World War II on Contemporary Jewish and Japanese American Communities," held in conjunction with the opening of the exhibition at Ellis Island, the late Egon Mayer, considered one of the most prominent chroniclers of American Jewry, opened his presentation with a joke.[1]

"Yom Kippur, the day of atonement, is the holiest of the Jewish holidays. One of the components of the liturgy is that the rabbi stands, confesses his sins, and acknowledges that he is a very lowly person, not worthy of God's forgiveness. So in this particular temple, the rabbi proceeds to do that, and there's a new cantor who sees this and figures maybe he ought to do something similar. So he gets up after the rabbi, prostrates himself, beats his breast, and says, "O God, I am lowly and unworthy of your forgiveness!" And after that, there is a sexton, who is a caretaker, and he feels this is a very nice thing to do so he gets up, prostrates himself, and weeps aloud, "O God, I am unworthy of your forgiveness!" And the cantor shoves his elbow into the rabbi's side and says, "Look who thinks he's unworthy!"

The point of Egon Mayer's joke is made clear later in this chapter. It is predicated upon knowing that in August 1995, Steven Briganti, the executive director of the Statue of Liberty–Ellis Island Foundation, had invited the Japanese American National Museum to mount America's

Concentration Camps at the Ellis Island Immigration Museum. The invitation to present the exhibition at such a prominent national and international landmark was a welcome opportunity to increase public awareness, especially because Ellis Island functioned as a little-known detention center for so-called enemy aliens during World War II. Yet, controversy regarding the use of the term "concentration camp" threatened this opportunity with censorship and raised questions about the American public's willingness to face its own history with the candor with which it has insisted that other nations face theirs.

In addition to the ten concentration camps and two isolation centers run by the War Relocation Authority (WRA), the sixteen assembly centers run by the Wartime Civil Control Administration, and eleven internment camps run by the Justice Department, there were more than twenty temporary detention facilities for enemy aliens run by various governmental agencies. Ellis Island was one of them. In 1942, an article in the *New York Times* reported, "For the time being, New York has a concentration camp of its own. It lies out in the harbor in the upper bay, beneath the green pepper-pot domes of the big Kremlin on Ellis Island."[2]

When the United States entered World War II, 121 Japanese were taken from their homes and businesses and shipped to Ellis Island. By mid-December 1941, there were 279 Japanese, 248 Germans, and 81 Italians interned at Ellis Island. Most of the Japanese were held from one to four months; a few were detained for up to two years. After their custody at Ellis Island, they were transferred to other detention centers, deported, or repatriated. By the end of 1944 the last of the Japanese internees were released, thus closing this little-known chapter of Ellis Island's history.

The exhibition designer, Ralph Appelbaum Associates, with T. Kevin Sayama as lead designer, worked with the National Museum's designer, Clement Hanami, to adapt the full-scale exhibition to a traveling version for the Ellis Island museum's designated space. Additional research on Ellis Island was conducted and incorporated into the exhibition. Funding was received from the Rockefeller Foundation. The National Museum's New York Advisory Council brought Japanese Americans together from the tristate area of New York, New Jersey, and Pennsylvania to help plan and to provide docents for this major event. Artifacts were gathered to reflect these local communities.

In mid-November 1997, five months before the scheduled opening, Appelbaum expressed concern to Briganti and the National Museum, noting: "There is an issue that has come to my attention from a number of sources which is that the title ACC [America's Concentration Camps] will be soundly criticized in the NY press as it implies a moral equivalency between the camps and ignores the current accepted meaning of concentration camps as death camps."[3] Since Cayleen Nakamura, the project manager, and I were scheduled to be in New York in early December, we took the opportunity to solicit feedback from a variety of individuals regarding this issue. While acknowledging the concerns, these individuals overwhelmingly supported keeping the original title and suggested that National Museum leaders meet with key individuals and organizations before the exhibition opened.

In January, the National Museum's executive director and CEO, Irene Hirano, spoke at the National Conference of Jewish Museums and took the opportunity to discuss the title and invite Jewish organizations in New York to work with the museum to cosponsor public programs. During that trip she also met with Briganti and Diane Dayson, superintendent of the Statue of Liberty National Monument, under which the Ellis Island Immigration Museum operates. Dayson told Hirano that she had received substantial expressions of concern from the National Park Service regional office about the use of the term "concentration camp" in the title, as well as concern over possible negative response by the Jewish community.[4]

On January 20, 1998, Dayson sent a facsimile addressed to me, which read in part: "The Park continues to strongly oppose the use of the words 'concentration camps' as a result of the most recent park exhibit and Smithsonian exhibit. This phrase today is used to refer to death camps; New York City has a very large Jewish community that could be offended by or misunderstand the use of this phrase. In addition, National Park Service superiors are not so inclined to endorse the title because of the controversy that stems around this title."[5]

Hirano asked me to respond to Dayson's message and to let Dayson know that the National Museum leaders had discussed this matter with many others and were confident that it was appropriate to keep the title. Hirano also wanted Dayson to know that we were planning a series of dialogues and programs prior to and during the show to further the educational mission of the exhibition.[6] In my letter to Dayson, I summarized the deliberation the museum had engaged in before the exhibition was first mounted. I explained that the National Museum fully recognized and respected the unique horror of the Holocaust and that we were aware that throughout history there have been many injustices, no one of which mitigates or draws equivalency to the others. In addition, I pointed out that it was critical for the Japanese American National Museum to address the semantics of suppression to underscore the broader lesson that when innocent Americans were herded into what the government itself called concentration camps, it was a failure of democracy that affects all Americans. I ended with the assurance that the museum would continue its original plans to discuss the issue with the Jewish leadership and other community leaders in New York.[7]

On February 4, after a conference call with Hirano and Briganti, Dayson sent Hirano a facsimile stating that "the word 'Concentration' must be removed from the title of your forthcoming exhibit if we are to install it on Ellis Island." She added, "Utilizing the words 'Concentration Camps' throughout the exhibit with an explanation of its meaning will be accepted. However, you must understand that should there be political pressure as a result of the words 'Concentration Camp' being used throughout the exhibit, there might be a chance that the park is requested to remove it."[8]

## Opening Up the Question

Given this mandate, the National Museum decided to open up the question to our constituents and colleagues, realizing it was a highly charged issue that would ultimately affect the Japanese American community at large and would have serious implications for the discipline of museology. The board of directors was immediately informed. We held open meetings with staff and volunteers. Hirano and board members contacted colleagues from the American Jewish community with whom we originally consulted four years earlier about the title and the use of the term. I contacted my original exhibit advisory committee as well as a variety of colleagues in the community, academe, and the museum field. After more than fifty years of historical neglect, the opportunity to tell the Japanese American story at such a highly visited landmark would be hard to sacrifice. But how much of the historical truth—as well as our commitment to refuting the euphemisms that have undermined this truth—would we be willing to compromise for this privilege?

Within forty-eight hours the museum staff heard from over a hundred people—including community members, American Jews, scholars, and museum professionals—by phone, e-mail, fax, and letters. Over the next few weeks, we heard from many others. Some felt that the term and title should be altered in order to attain the larger goal of educating others about the camp experience. Dr. Harry Abe, a member of the National Museum's board of governors, wrote, "Rather than being turned down completely by insisting on the word 'concentration' we can avoid a confrontation and soften the word by choosing another."[9] Grant Ujifusa, another member of the board of governors, called and said, "I think we should go ahead and call it 'America's Internment Camps'—a rose by any other name is still a rose. It's silly to give up something over a semantic matter."[10]

The majority of those who contacted us, however, urged us to keep the original title and not bow to pressure. There were many reasons provided. For some—former inmates decrying their right to discard the euphemisms that had covered up the injustice—it was personally alarming. Aiko Herzig-Yoshinaga, an independent researcher and former inmate, sent a letter saying, "At what point are we, as Americans of Japanese ancestry, going to cease to resist having our history written for us by others? Is our empowerment so weak that we must capitulate and surrender our right to state our own history in our own words? . . . If the cc words are unacceptable in the title, why would they be acceptable in the text labels and what assurance is there that you would not be asked to remove them later also?"[11] Masako and Richard Murakami, longtime National Museum volunteers, wrote, "We strongly oppose any form of censorship which will result in the removal of the words 'concentration camp' from the exhibit. . . . Our parents, also U.S. citizens, being law-abiding persons, went quietly to be imprisoned behind barbed wire. . . . Removal of the words 'concentration camp' is an attempt to change this historical fact. . . . The Japanese American experience must be told as it actually happened—incarceration of United States citizens in American concentration camps."[12]

For others it was a larger academic and professional concern. Lonnie Bunch, then associate director for curatorial affairs at the National Museum of American History, wrote, "As an African American scholar and a senior museum professional, I feel that it is inappropriate and quite dangerous for any educational institution to dictate the interpretive posture of an exhibition to those who have studied, analyzed, and mastered the subject."[13] Professor Lamont Yeakey of California State University, Los Angeles, specified, "I urge you to stand true to your beliefs and stick with the correct title of your exhibit. . . . Moreover, not to use the term would undermine historical accuracy and gravely distort the reality of this tragic event."[14]

Several scholars referred to the redress and reparations movement organized by the Japanese American community that resulted in a hard-won apology and compensation from the U.S. government for its wrongful actions during World War II.[15] The historian Arthur Hansen emphatically declared, "There should be no compromise on the terminology. The slippage would be a form of accommodation that the Japanese American community participated in under duress in the past. The redress effort was an attempt to get over that. To flip back into it would be to capitulate to a historic falsification. 'Concentration camp' is a decidedly accurate term."[16] Mitchell T. Maki wrote, "A community is only as strong as its members' desire to maintain it. Self-definition is a central component to the maintenance of a community. Let us not have won the battle for redress only to sacrifice its true achievement: the Japanese American community's willingness to tell their own story of a terrible injustice and the subsequent recognition of that injustice by the United States government."[17]

For some Jewish scholars, it was also a source of deep anguish. Tom

Freudenheim, executive director of the Yivo Institute for Jewish Research, exclaimed, "My first reaction is one of deep embarrassment! As a Jew, born in Hitler's Germany, who lost various relatives in the Holocaust, I am deeply disturbed by the notion that Jewish Americans appear to be telling Japanese Americans about sensitivity." Freudenheim said further that the internment of Japanese Americans "may not be comparable to the decimation of my people, but I certainly don't feel that should prevent us from recognizing, and naming, America's concentration camps as precisely what they were: concentration camps."[18] Professor Egon Mayer wrote:

> That a public official of the United States in 1998 would seek to censor history in such a virtually extortionary manner is appalling in the extreme. What makes this matter all the more disturbing to me personally is that Ms. Dayson, Superintendent of the Statue of Liberty National Monument, appears to be compelling the change in title in the name of New York's "large Jewish community that could be offended" by the use of the phrase "concentration camp" as applied to the Japanese experience. Such reasoning is an outrageous incitement to completely unwarranted intergroup animosity. In my opinion Ms. Dayson has succeeded in offending both the Japanese and Jewish American community in one thoughtless gesture.[19]

## Working toward Resolution

Because the Ellis Island Museum is part of the National Park Service, and with only six weeks remaining before the scheduled exhibition installation, the chair of the National Museum's board of governors, Senator Daniel K. Inouye, appealed personally and directly to Bruce Babbitt, secretary of the interior. Inouye's letter, dated February 5, 1998, began, "After much thought and consideration, I decided to communicate with you on a matter of great importance to me." Inouye summarized the World War II incarceration of Japanese Americans and indicated that a year and a half previously the museum had begun discussions with the Ellis Island Foundation to host the exhibition. He pointed out, "The title of the exhibit was always visible on all materials previewed by the

Ellis Island Foundation, and in the course of the many times that the Museum staff met with the National Park Service staff, it was no secret that the title of the exhibit was 'America's Concentration Camps.'" He wrote that as chair of the National Museum's board of governors, he had personally discussed the exhibition, including the term "concentration camp," with numerous leaders from both the Japanese American and American Jewish communities. He quoted at length from my letter to Dayson, which he introduced by saying, "I wish to share with you a few paragraphs of this letter which I believe clearly sets forth my position and that of my Board."[20]

The next day the senator informed the museum staff that Secretary Babbitt would investigate the matter and get back to him within a week's time. The senator sent a copy of his letter to Babbitt to the Conference of Presidents of Major American Jewish Organizations as well as to the Israeli ambassador. Secretary of Transportation Norman Mineta, a member of the National Museum's board of trustees, spoke to Secretary Babbitt on our behalf, as did Senator Daniel Akaka of Hawai'i.

During this same time there was continued and considerable activity on both coasts by many people. National Museum staff, board members, New York Advisory Council members, and volunteers conducted formal and informal meetings with American Jewish leaders and organizations such as the Museum of Jewish Heritage in New York, the American Jewish Committee, the Simon Wiesenthal Center in Los Angeles, and the Holocaust Memorial Museum in Washington, D.C. Rose Ochi, then director of the U.S. Department of Justice Community Relations Service Center in Washington, D.C., informed Chantale Wong, chief of staff to John Garamendi, deputy secretary of the interior, about the issue.[21] Many colleagues, National Museum staff, volunteers, board members, and people from the community voiced their opinions. Because of their expertise of the subject, long-standing commitment to justice, and experience in community organization, Bruce Iwasaki and Phil Taijitsu Nash, who are both attorneys, were particularly helpful.

As a member of the historical advisory council to Ellis Island, the historian Roger Daniels was especially alarmed because the council had not been informed or consulted about this issue. He contacted Dwight

Pitcaithley, chief historian of the National Park Service, who also said he knew nothing of the matter. Daniels urged the museum not to make any irrevocable decisions until hearing from Pitcaithley. With good humor, Daniels concluded his memo by observing that "obviously, a Friday is not always the best time to start to move the federal bureaucracy."[22] However, Dwight Pitcaithley called me the next morning (a Saturday) at my home to let me know he was looking into the matter and emphasized that he could speak for the national office in saying that the park service, as a public agency, cannot adhere to any specific point of view, that all perspectives need to and should be discussed openly.

I included his remarks in a report on the issue to the National Museum's board of trustees at its meeting later that day. The controversy evoked different opinions among board members. Robert Volk admitted he was uncomfortable with the term "concentration camp." Dr. Margaret Oda felt that in the interest of education, we should not lose the opportunity to be exhibited at this iconic national site. Bruce Kaji, George Takei, and Norman Mineta—themselves former inmates of the World War II camps—felt the museum needed to hold firm to the original title and not again be coerced by the U.S. government. Mel Chiogioji, a retired rear admiral, simply stated that the museum could not let an outside entity tell it what to do. Because the issue had been placed before Secretary Babbitt and Chief Historian Pitcaithley, both of whom indicated they would look into the matter, the board decided to await their responses before determining what action the museum would take.

On February 13, eight days after Senator Inouye's letter to Secretary Babbitt, Irene Hirano received a call from Diane Dayson indicating that there would be no restriction on the title of the show and that the traveling exhibition could go forward as originally planned. We felt victorious and relieved. On a practical level, the curatorial, design, fabrication, education, marketing, and public programs teams all went into overdrive to make up for lost time. On a larger sociological and political level, the decision meant that the threat of censorship was just that, a threat only, and that amicable intergroup discussions could resume as planned—or so we thought.

Secretary Babbitt's chief of staff assigned this issue to Jacqueline

Lowey, deputy to Robert Stanton, director of the National Park Service, and she assisted museum staff in carrying out our original plan to meet with American Jewish leaders and organizations in New York to discuss the issue face-to-face. The national office of the American Jewish Committee (AJC) was asked to host a meeting with representatives of a variety of American Jewish and Japanese American organizations in New York. Jeffrey Weintraub, from the AJC's Belfer Center for American Pluralism, was assigned to organize this meeting, which was scheduled for March 9, 1998.

## Making Headlines

On February 26, 1998—ten days before the meeting—an article by J. J. Goldberg appeared in about a dozen Jewish newspapers across the country with the headline, "Jews, Japanese Clash over Holocaust Language."[23] The tone of the article was framed by its opening sentence: "Jewish and Japanese American community leaders are headed for what could become a bruising confrontation." The article reported that "Dayson declined to be interviewed and won't say who or what prompted her to spring her threat on the Japanese Americans in January barely two months before the show[']s opening." Journalistically, the article provided insight into the issue at hand, reporting that "several officials say the park service has been skittish since another furor at Ellis Island last fall when an exhibit on the 1915 massacre of Armenians in Turkey had to be revised in midseason, following Turkish protests." However, using language such as "the Jewish-Japanese feud has become a tug-of-war between two successful ethnic groups, both trying to establish their status as history's victims," the article also did exactly what the National Museum did not want, which was to have the incident misrepresented and sensationalized as a squabble between two American ethnic groups.

On March 8, 1998, the day before our meeting with New York Jewish and Japanese American leaders, New York's mainstream newspapers picked up the story. The *New York Times* headline inquired, "What Is a Concentration Camp? Ellis Island Exhibit Prompts a Debate." While presenting both sides of the issue, the article incisively stated, "But the debate clearly goes beyond the semantic, touching on the questions of how to remember a people's suffering and who has the right to tell that story."[24] *New York Newsday*'s headline similarly queried, "Who Defines 'Concentration Camp'?"[25]

## The Meeting

The March 9 meeting had been well publicized. The American Jewish Committee reported that more people called wanting to attend than it could accommodate. In the end, twenty-four people attended, including representatives from the National Foundation for Jewish Culture, Jewish Council for Public Affairs, Anti-Defamation League, American Gathering of Jewish Holocaust Survivors, New York Jewish Community Relations Council, American Jewish Congress, and the Japanese American Citizens League.[26] Martin Bresler of the AJC's Belfer Center for American Pluralism chaired the meeting.

Senator Inouye told the group that even among the casualties and the loss of human life he experienced during the war, three noncombat-related incidents changed his life forever. First, after the nation of Japan bombed Pearl Harbor, he and all Nisei were reclassified 4-C, which designated them "enemy aliens," an accusation that gravely insulted him then and now. Second, after having volunteered for the segregated, all–Japanese American 442nd Regimental Combat Team, he and other Nisei soldiers visited Rohwer, one of the ten American concentration camps. The gravity of the experience left him asking himself if he would have volunteered to serve in the U.S. Army from behind barbed wire—a question, he said, that haunts him to this day. Third, while in the hospital in Atlantic City in June 1945, recuperating from his battlefield wounds, he met a fellow Japanese American soldier who served in the 522nd Field Artillery Battalion, which liberated one of the satellite camps of Dachau. This soldier told Inouye firsthand of the horrors he encountered there. Remembering the effect of that conversation over twenty years later, the senator had introduced a bill to repeal Title II of the Emergency Detention Act of 1950, which provided the power

Those attending the meeting on March 9, 1998, at the offices of the American Jewish Committee (AJC) in New York included (left to right) Karen Ishizuka, Senator Daniel K. Inouye, and Irene Hirano, JANM; Martin Bresler, AJC's Belfer Center for American Pluralism; Norman Mineta, JANM; Shula Bahat, AJC; Michi Weglyn, author; and Jeffrey Weintraub, AJC's Belfer Center for American Pluralism.

to erect domestic camps for individuals suspected of being threats to national security. The senator ended his comments by saying that we—Japanese Americans and American Jews—should be working together, and that together we could prevent the question of who might be next from ever arising.

David Harris, executive director of the American Jewish Committee, responded that he had no disagreement with what had been said. He noted that, indeed, the Japanese American Citizens League had given the American Jewish Committee an award for its support during the

Japanese American campaign to obtain redress and reparations from the U.S. government. He said that the AJC had not approached the Ellis Island museum, the National Park Service, or the Department of the Interior to oppose use of the term and had not initiated a call to the media to bring attention to or exert pressure on this matter. He said it was not the exhibition that he found problematic, adding, "let a thousand such exhibits bloom." But he and others were seriously concerned about the use of the term "concentration camp" outside the Jewish experience. He stated that while Jews were not the first to use it, the term "concentration camp" automatically conjured up images of starvation and experimentation specific to the Holocaust and thereby had taken on a new level of meaning.

The discussion proceeded with expressions of respect for each group's past and mutual concern for the present and future. Norman Mineta brought up the dire need for education concerning Asian Americans. He stated that Americans of Asian descent were still not perceived or treated as Americans even after generations in this country, adding that he is still complimented on how well he speaks English and asked how long he has been in this country. Everyone agreed that it was important for future generations to learn from history, to remember the past. The only point of contention was the term "concentration camp."

Benjamin Meed, president of the American Gathering of Jewish Holocaust Survivors, offered a pragmatic solution. He said he knew Japanese Americans were not trying to equate their experience with the horrors of the Holocaust but that the use of the term would be a problem. He proposed that an explanation—jointly authored—distinguishing the Nazi death camps from the American concentration camps be placed at the beginning of the exhibition. In this way the public would be further educated and it would be clear to all that no equivalency was intended. His suggestion was embraced by all in attendance, and Stephen Steinlight and Kenneth Stern of the American Jewish Committee and I were charged with crafting the statement. Four hours later we came up with the following text. It was adopted with some minor changes and placed at the beginning of the exhibition, not only at Ellis Island but at every venue.

A concentration camp is a place where people are imprisoned not because of any crimes they committed, but simply because of who they are. Although many groups have been singled out for such persecution throughout history, the term "concentration camps" was first used at the turn of the century in the Spanish American and Boer Wars.

During World War II, America's concentration camps were clearly distinguishable from Nazi Germany's. Nazi camps were places of torture, barbarous medical experiments, and summary executions; some were extermination centers with gas chambers. Six million Jews and many others, including Gypsies, Poles, homosexuals, and political dissidents were slaughtered in the Holocaust.

In recent years, concentration camps have existed in the former Soviet Union, Cambodia, and Bosnia.

Despite the difference, all had one thing in common: the people in power removed a minority group from the general population and the rest of society let it happen.

## Nationwide Discussion and Debate

After the meeting, an editor from the *New York Times* contacted me to ask my thoughts on the meeting. The next day the *Times* and *New York Newsday* carried follow-up articles announcing that an accord had been reached.[27] The *New York Times* editorial reported: "If the title was intended to shock, it has succeeded. Some American Jewish groups have strongly objected, arguing that the term has become indelibly associated with the Holocaust and would be cheapened by being used in this way. Their concern that the Holocaust be remembered as a uniquely vile expression of human evil is a reasonable one. But it does no service to the memory of the victims of Nazi genocide to distort an ugly truth about American history." The editorial concluded by saying, "Calling the American camps what American leaders themselves called them does not diminish the horror of the Holocaust or equate the persecution of Japanese Americans with genocide. There is a value to preserving the continuity of language even when it is a painful thing to do."[28]

Over the next few days and weeks came a flurry of letters to the editor, more articles in mainstream newspapers such as the *Washington*

*Times,* and many articles, editorials, and letters in local and national American Jewish and Japanese American newspapers regarding the controversy.[29] Martin Lapidus, in a letter to the *Jewish Week* stated, "I find it incredibly arrogant that leaders of some Jewish organizations think that the words 'concentration camps' ('War of Words,' Feb. 23) are a registered preserve solely limited to Jews."[30] To the *Jewish Journal,* the late Fred Okrand, an attorney for the American Civil Liberties Union, wrote, "It retreats not one whit from the horrors of the Nazi camps to recognize what the American camps were. It belittles us if we deny the truth."[31] The debate was even reported in the German publication *Der Spiegel.*[32]

That so many people were suddenly buzzing over America's concentration camps and why the term should or should not be used is in itself significant. It is ironic that America's concentration camps provoked such public dialogue some fifty years after the fact when the public at large was so disturbingly silent when the camps were in use. In the July 29, 1942, issue of the *Christian Century,* Norman Thomas wrote, "In an experience of nearly three decades I have never found it harder to arouse the American public on any important issue than on this. Men and women who know nothing of the facts . . . hotly deny that there are concentration camps."[33]

Suddenly, this brief but intense episode stimulated serious and often emotional dialogue among historians, sociologists, cultural workers, Americans of Japanese ancestry, American Jews, and other ethnic communities in deeply meaningful and even unsettling ways. It spurred a rousing debate and difference of opinion within both the American Jewish and Japanese American communities. Such intragroup discord is a reminder that these groups are not homogeneous entities that can be generalized or stereotyped but are composed of highly distinctive and often divergent individuals. Articles and letters to editors written by American Jews and Japanese Americans signified the disparity within, as well as the heartfelt passions of, both groups. Clyde Haberman in his *New York Times* column claimed, "This compromise does not alter the fact that many Jews fear they are losing their singular lexicon of anguish: words like 'ghetto,' 'genocide,' 'Diaspora' and the most power-

*Der Spiegel* covered the 1998 controversy over use of the term "concentration camp" at the Ellis Island Immigration Museum. Courtesy of *Der Spiegel*.

packed of all: 'Holocaust.' Every one has been appropriated by others, notably American blacks, who have recognized the sheer force of this vocabulary and have harnessed it to describe their own history of suffering and bloodshed."[34] Conversely, Jonathan Mark in the *Jewish Week* stated, "Thumbs down to Jews protesting against Japanese Americans for the linguistic trespass of saying they were put, during wartime, into 'concentration camps.' . . . It was to our glory that the biblical language of Jewish slavery was appropriated by black slaves. . . . It's Jewish malpractice to monopolize pain and minimize victims. We, of all people, should be first in line to comfort the 'concentrated.'"[35]

Similar differences in opinion existed within the Japanese American community. In the newspaper of the Japanese American Citizens League, the *Pacific Citizen*, two letters to the editor criticized the National

Museum's stance, but from very different perspectives. John Nishio felt it was unnecessary to add the jointly authored definition of "concentration camp" to the exhibition: "The exhibit about the Japanese American camps is not about Jews and no footnote is required. . . . Adding footnotes about Jewish history to such an exhibit derogates the experience of JA's. The footnote at the exhibit should be expunged. I implore those responsible to please retract the generous, but unnecessary, offer to include the footnote."[36] Mas Odoi specifically reprimanded me while reiterating a traditionalistic compliance shared by many:

> Senior curator of the exhibit Karen Ishizuka evidently does not know that the relocation centers were a means of dispersing those of Japanese ancestry from the military zones along the Pacific Coast to inland areas. Japanese Americans of proven loyalty left the camps in large numbers because that is the only way they would be accepted in their new homes in the east. . . . But it was an understandable mistake during the exigencies of a war for national survival. . . . Isn't it time for us JAs to realize that ours is an outstanding American success story that has international and historic repercussions?[37]

Toru Miyoshi supported the joint statement to clarify concentration camps from Nazi Germany's death camps but suggested the following sentence be added: "We had one thing that was uncommon: the tragic Jewish experience occurred under a dictatorship while the illegal incarceration of Japanese Americans happened in our democracy."[38]

## The Lesson of Egon Mayer

At the public program in New York, Egon Mayer prefaced his remarks by saying that telling a joke—particularly a Jewish one in a multicultural setting—was risky. From the warm laughter his joke elicited, he had to admit, "I guess it worked, right?" Having enchanted the audience, he went on to devastate us with the story of his own experience during World War II.

His family was from Hungary and was among a small group of Jews who, for complex reasons, managed to escape the death camps. After the war, they went back to Hungary, where they learned about the losses various families had suffered. Whenever his family relayed what had happened to them—whether to other Jewish families, acquaintances, friends, or even relatives—the almost predictable and uniform response was one of not quite disparagement, not quite disbelief, but an accusation of, "How could you complain about your suffering when you are alive?"

In 1963, his father was asked to testify at the trial of one of the Germans involved in their rescue. Members of the prosecution team were aghast that a Jew would give objective, honest testimony that ultimately supported an ex-Nazi. His father returned from the trial saying, "You know, I felt that they would have rather we died." Mayer said that he has only recently come to grips with the feeling he sensed through his youth and adult life, "that there are multitudes of others who lost families who would have rather the rest of us died as well."

> And that's a very painful thing to acknowledge. And in thinking about the Japanese American experience and the concentration camps in the United States, of course they were not death camps and of course people were not treated the way Nazis treated Jews. But I think it would be lamentable if the only way that we can feel another's pain is if they experience the same magnitude of suffering. That would, I am afraid, reduce us to the level of our victimizers. I think we want to be able to recognize that there are multitudes of ways to suffer and the sufferers are always worthy at least of each other's forgiveness, if not of God's.

He concluded by saying that the lesson of American Jews and Japanese Americans coming together and coming to terms with these moments in history was for us to not only share with one another but "to illuminate to the rest of the world just how it is possible to both suffer and survive and that the differences in no way diminish the evil that motivated the infliction of that suffering."[39]

• • •

Despite the threat of censorship and spirited public debate over its title, the exhibition opened in New York on April 3, 1998, intact and on time. Contrary to the warning that it could be shut down, the exhibition was extended beyond its intended closing date and did not end until January 31, 1999. The only change to the original exhibition was the addition of the definition of the term "concentration camp" crafted by the AJC and the National Museum. This definition became a permanent and important part of the exhibition as it traveled to Atlanta, San Francisco, and Little Rock.

It was clear from the discussion that swirled about the debate that the real issue was not a question of terminology nor was it a Japanese American–American Jewish problem. The public dialogues had transcended the title, the exhibition itself, and even the goal of educating others about America's concentration camps. Rather, the questions that had been evoked—about historical perspective, censorship, the free expression of ideas, and our own prejudices—were by far more profound than the problem at hand or the solution we came up with. What becomes "history" and from whose point of view? How do you encourage people to explore its dark chapters and come away even stronger? Why remember when you would just as soon forget?

# 8 / Recovering History and Recovering *from* History

I had known this man for years. He was a successful businessman and a recognized leader in the community. While I had talked with many Nisei who shy away from discussing their camp experience, this man was not one of them. On the contrary, he was one of the few of his generation who spoke early, often, and out loud about the injustices of camp and the necessity to remember so that such an event never occur again. He spoke never out of bitterness but out of a conviction that comes from those who know. So when I set up a meeting with him to obtain his input about the exhibition, I was startled to see that as we talked—one on one—he started to shake. "After all these years," he mustered, "while intellectually I know we did nothing wrong, I still feel ashamed."

While the Japanese American National Museum's goal was to produce an introductory exhibition on the camps for a broad audience, my challenge as its curator and as a Sansei was also to make it meaningful for those whose experience this was. I was faced with two seemingly disparate audiences: a general audience, many of whom would know little or nothing about this chapter of American history, and an intimate audience whose members not only were the ones incarcerated, but for whom "camp" in all its nuances and resonance had become fundamental to their very identity. Although these two audiences were seemingly different, in the process of curating the exhibition I came to the conclusion that they were not only linked, but that each served to illuminate the other. A general audience can be provided with facts and figures; however, only by understanding the meaning of camp from the inmates' perspective could the public at large begin to understand the depth of its significance. And conversely, because camp has been a source of humiliation to the former inmates for so many decades, public recognition of their experience is critical to their ability to come to grips with the event that forever after dichotomized their lives into "before the war" and "after the war." In essence, recovering history involves recovering *from* history.

### Recovering History

The curatorial strategy of adopting and manifesting the inmates' perspective resulted in the discovery of extraordinary items that had been unknown and unseen for decades. Tucked away—sometimes neatly and sometimes haphazardly—for some fifty years, a cornucopia of photographs, documents, letters, and stories came tumbling out of people's garages and closets when it became known we were looking for artifacts for the exhibition. Some items were related to known figures and incidents; others were marvelously new and unique.

We were able to exhibit only a portion of the objects that were brought forth. Some were borrowed for the exhibition and returned. Many were donated to the National Museum, where they are being preserved for generations to come and call out for scholarly attention. Several documents that were displayed in the exhibition were difficult to appreciate fully when they were under glass and are worth presenting here. The following artifacts demonstrate that, despite the government's rationale and the media's corroboration, members of the Japanese American community were acutely aware of the undemocratic nature of the issues and events. Although they had little choice at the time but to comply with Executive Order 9066, they were not as submissive as we may have thought.

## Joe Kurihara Statement

In the Manzanar display was a thirty-two-page handwritten statement by Joe Kurihara, a former World War I veteran who vociferously opposed the incarceration. His life history was included in the earliest study of the incarceration, conducted in 1942. The results were published in a book entitled *The Spoilage,* where Kurihara's experience was used to illustrate "the cumulative impact of circumstances in transforming attitudes of 'loyalty' to those of 'disloyalty.'"[1]

Born in Kauai in 1895, Kurihara moved to California, enlisted in the U.S. Army, and served abroad before returning, attending college, and becoming a successful businessman. When World War II broke out he tried to offer his services to the war effort only to be turned down because of his ancestry. Although he had no interest in or connection to Japan before the incarceration, after General John L. DeWitt of the Western Defense Command expressed the pervasive U.S. military attitude that "a Jap's a Jap," Kurihara "swore to become a Jap 100 percent."[2] In Manzanar he became active in anti-administration and anti-JACL activity. Arrested during the Manzanar riot on December 7, 1942, Kurihara was sent to the isolation camp in Moab, Utah, and later Leupp, Arizona, and then transferred to Tule Lake, California, where he renounced his citizenship and was deported to Japan.

Although considered "subversive" and "anti-American," one WRA officer concluded, "I find Joe Kurihara very bitter about the entire situation, but he is bitter and sore in quite an American way."[3] Within the handwritten statement displayed in the exhibition, Kurihara challenged, "I, for one, have gone over there [Europe] and have fought to save Democracy. Where is that Democracy today?"[4]

## Minoru Yasui Poem

Unlike Manzanar, Minidoka in Idaho has been one of the less recognized camps, except to its 9,397 inhabitants. So I was gratified to find many artifacts of historical as well as personal interest connected to Minidoka. One of them was a poem written by Minoru Yasui, a Nisei attorney who resigned from the Japanese consulate in Chicago when

Pearl Harbor was bombed and later challenged the legality of the forced removal and detention of Japanese Americans.

After the exclusion orders were issued in February 1942, a curfew law was passed that required all persons of Japanese ancestry to be indoors between 8 P.M. and 6 A.M. Because it was based on race, Yasui deliberately set out to challenge the law and, on the night of March 28, 1942, entered a police station in Portland, Oregon, at midnight, demanding to be arrested. Yasui ended up serving nine months in prison and taking his case to the Supreme Court.[5] *Yasui v. United States* was one of four Supreme Court cases that contested the legality of detaining people solely on the basis of race. While each case was different and complex, the constitutionality of both the curfew and exclusion orders was eventually upheld. In 1981 it was discovered that evidence had been suppressed and the individuals' convictions were overturned.

Yasui wrote the poem that was displayed while he was incarcerated in Minidoka. He sent it to his father, Masuo Yasui, who was detained in a Justice Department internment camp in Santa Fe, New Mexico. Masuo Yasui, in turn, carefully copied it into a scrapbook on March 24, 1943—a year to the month after his son deliberately violated the curfew law. Yasui's poem ends with, "If freedom is to survive, if democracy of all / men is to live again, / Your high sense of justice and your national / self-respect you must regain!!!"[6]

### The Mothers' Society of Minidoka

One of the most astounding documents discovered was a two-page typewritten letter to President Franklin D. Roosevelt from an organization called the Mothers' Society of Minidoka, asking that the drafting of Japanese American men be suspended until their civil rights were reinstated.[7] The letter not only defies stereotypes of the placid Nisei, especially that of the supposedly more compliant Nisei woman, but also shows that these individuals had the grit and gumption to speak out against what they saw was wrong and to appeal to the highest authority.

In the letter they refer to current events such as the reclassification of Nisei men to 4-C, which made them ineligible for the draft, revealing that these women were well informed and not simply speaking from emotion. Although common knowledge now, they pointed out then that "despite General DeWitt's proclamation that 'a Jap's a Jap' there had been no case of sabotage by Japanese Americans." The letter also reflects a sophisticated level of political interpretation. They write that "on the Pacific Coast with the so-called 'military necessity' as reason, the foundation of our life, the fruit of several decades of toil and suffering, was overturned." By inserting the adjective "so-called" and positioning the phrase "military necessity" in quotation marks, the members of the Mothers' Society show that they clearly did not believe that was the real reason for their incarceration.

On March 14, 1944, a letter of response was issued on behalf of the president from the Selective Service System. The Mothers' Society evidently has left no stone unturned as the rebuttal first acknowledged "similar letters addressed to the Secretary of War and to the Director of Selective Service on the same subject" that they had sent. Conflating the draft with a civil right, the letter addresses the mothers' request by stating, "This obligation, however, for military service in time of war is both a duty and a privilege of American citizens." The letter ends with the rebuke, "Your cooperation in this process will assist you individually and will hasten the day when a full and satisfactory solution to this problem for all concerned may be obtained."[8]

## Continuing Acts of Historical Recovery

During the course of the exhibition, more artifacts, documents, photographs, and insights continued to pour in, including vital information about items displayed. This ongoing collaboration between the curator and the community is, in essence, testimony to the community's functioning as curator.

### Yoshio Okumoto, Heart Mountain Photographer

The opening panel of the exhibition featured a striking photographic panorama of throngs of inmates at Heart Mountain, Wyoming (see chapter 4). The picture of this mass of humanity arrayed against rows of barracks provided a powerful symbol of the forced removal and incarceration. It was originally found in a scrapbook that had been donated to the museum, but the photographer remained unknown until four months into the exhibition when Mamoru Inouye of Los Gatos, California, wrote that the photograph, as well as the panorama that formed the 10' × 30' billboard outside the museum, had been taken by Yoshio Okumoto.[9]

Inouye included photocopies of the front and back of the photographs, which revealed that the billboard photo was taken on March 28, 1943, at f16 at 1/50 second with a red filter. The photograph we used at the exhibition entrance was taken on September 21, 1943, at 1:30 P.M. at f19, 1/25 second, and bore the notation, "Segregation Program—Tule Lake bound, 1st contingent gathering at High School Bldg."[10]

A billboard that was part of the outdoor exhibition featured a photograph of Heart Mountain taken by Yoshio Okumoto. Photograph by Norman H. Sugimoto.

Inouye included an article on Okumoto, published in November 1987, so we might also know a little about the person behind the photographs.[11] Okumoto left his home in Hilo, Hawai'i, for California in 1923. A few years later he was admitted to Stanford University in California, where he worked in the anatomy department preparing slides. After graduation he also became the live-in caretaker of the Japanese Student Association's clubhouse on campus. When Executive Order 9066 removed all Japanese Americans from the West Coast, Okumoto packed and stored the clubhouse's belongings, among which would be a windfall that would benefit the university decades later.

Okumoto was incarcerated at Heart Mountain for three and a half years. When the ban on cameras in camp was lifted, he sent for his camera and became the camp's de facto photographer. He built a darkroom in the barracks he shared with seven other bachelors, and he ordered photographic supplies from the Sears and Montgomery Ward catalogues. After the war Okumoto returned to Stanford to work. In 1985, members of the prewar Japanese Student Association held a reunion and Okumoto made the startling announcement that the association's two bank accounts had been accumulating interest since 1942 and now totaled $27,500. The group decided to donate the money to Stanford for a scholarship fund for Japanese American students. Okumoto retired from Stanford a year later, having served the university, except for his years in camp, from 1927 to 1986. Okumoto passed away on February 16, 1993, at the age of ninety. Inouye ended his letter with, "I bring this information to your attention with the hopes that Yoshio Okumoto will receive due credit for his photographic work."

## Heart Mountain Mystery Rocks

One of the great finds—and great mysteries—was literally unearthed during the development of the exhibition. It was a group of small rocks, each carefully inscribed with a Japanese character (*kanji*). In March 1994, the filmmaker Emiko Omori of San Francisco came in with six of the stones. I took them to my friend Rinban Noriaki Ito, of the neighboring Higashi Hongwanji Betsuin, as Richard Drinnon had written about similar stones whose characters were thought to be fragments of Buddhist sutras.[12] Rinban Ito and his secretary, Mary Imoto, were able to translate five of the six and indicated that because the characters needed to be analyzed in context with the others, it was possible they were part of the sutras, although some could also be read as family names. They could also tell, by the handwriting, that they were written by different people.

In June 1994, Nancy Araki traveled to Wyoming to coordinate the transport of the Heart Mountain barracks, as described in chapter 3, and there she met Les and Nora Bovee. The Bovees were the homesteaders who, it turned out, had given the stones to both Omori and Drinnon. After the closing of the Heart Mountain camp in November 1945, the site was made available to homesteading. In the late 1940s, on the Bovee property, a bulldozer accidentally uncovered a 55-gallon oil drum filled with 656 rocks, each with a Japanese character written on it with black ink. The Bovees donated the oil drum and its contents to the National Museum.[13]

In the first issue of the *Japanese American National Museum Quarterly*, an article dubbed the stones the "Heart Mountain mystery rocks" and issued a query: "If you have information about the Heart Mountain stones, please share it with us and join in the Museum's ongoing commitment to learning more about, and telling the diverse stories of Americans of Japanese ancestry."[14]

About twenty stones were displayed in the exhibition. The accompanying caption said that while the origins of the calligraphed rocks remained a mystery, they were thought to be parts of Buddhist sutras. In April 1999, after seeing the stones in the exhibition, Shinjiro Kanazawa of San Diego, California, helped solve the puzzle of the Heart Mountain "mystery rocks." He sent the museum a letter pointing out that when a child died, grieving parents would write passages from sutras—and sometimes their children's names—on pebbles and build the stones into piles in order to help the deceased safely enter the other world.[15] According to Kanazawa, the folk belief is that between this world and the next there is a "children's limbo"; when a deceased child succeeds at building a tower of pebbles in this limbo, Jizo, the guardian deity of children, appears to help the child across the river and safely onto the

Rocks bearing Japanese characters discovered at Heart Mountain. Collection of JANM, gift of Leslie and Nora Bovee (94.158.1). Photograph by Norman H. Sugimoto.

other shore. Keeping with the folk belief, Kanazawa concluded, "I also suggest that you at least repose the souls of babies that the pebbles were gathered for, before you exhibit them."

## Another Child of Manzanar

At the opening of America's Concentration Camps, Mary Seko of Chatsworth, California, saw a Caucasian girl amidst the Nisei children in the video *Something Strong Within*. Seko wrote to me a few months later with information about Erica Harth, a Caucasian woman who had been a child in Manzanar.[16] Although the girl in the video was not Harth, Seko included a heartfelt article from the *Massachusetts Review* written by Harth, now a professor at Brandeis University in Massachusetts.[17] While the main focus of the exhibition was to tell the story of the camps from the inmates' perspective, the overarching mission of the National Museum is to position this historic episode as a significant part of American, not just Japanese American, history. Therefore I was glad to know of Harth's personal history and that camp had an emotional resonance for her.

In 1944, when she was five years old, Harth spent a year in camp. Her mother worked for the WRA as a relocation counselor to help inmates in the resettlement process after they were released. Harth recalled, "The administrative section where we lived was literally white. Its white painted bungalows stared across at the rows of brown tarpaper barracks that housed the internees."[18] The article she wrote demonstrates that, like her Japanese American counterparts, she was greatly affected by camp. It took years of reflection, a lot of research, and a pilgrimage across the country back to Manzanar for her to understand how.

Recalling a story of a Nisei boy in camp who begged to be taken "back to America," Harth writes, "I think I knew that I was in 'America.' It is only now, as I realize how firmly the year of residence at Manzanar has sedimented my identity, that I wonder. . . . What I saw of the war was an *American* concentration camp for people who, it was later confirmed, committed no wartime act of sabotage or espionage."[19]

In 1992, Harth traveled back to California to attend the Manzanar Pilgrimage, an annual event that began in 1969 to commemorate the camps. In the process she located several former classmates, formed new friendships, and even agreed to speak about her personal connection to Manzanar at the open microphone on the bus ride back to Los Angeles. "It did not take me long to realize that in a curiously logical way I am something of an insider among the survivors of Manzanar," she later wrote. "My residence at the camp, my attendance at its school allow me to bear witness to the event as few other *hakujin* can." And yet Harth acknowledges that her experience was fundamentally different than that of her classmates. The 1992 pilgrimage ended with collective congratulations on Manzanar's hard-won status as a national historic site and the success of the redress movement. "But to me," Harth wrote, "undeniably an outsider to the internment, words of celebration came uneasily."[20] "On the flimsiest of pretexts," she recalled, "ten thousand people were jammed into the small plot of land that made such a puny cell for them and such a large playground for me."[21]

## Resolutions Regarding the Draft

In January 1996, Jogi Yamaguchi, a museum volunteer, came in with a faded mimeographed document entitled, "Resolutions to the War Department from Delegates of Manzanar Draft Age Citizens."[22] Like the letter to Roosevelt from the Mothers' Society of Minidoka, this piece illustrated that the incarcerated Nisei did not simply accept their plight with resignation but actively tried to restore American democracy from the bottom up.

A cover letter with the document, directed to the director of Manzanar, revealed that the authors of the resolution were representatives of draft-age males elected by their respective block who "have, at times, wondered whether the principles of democracy upon which our nation is founded are real and existent." The letter stated further, "But withal, we still cling firmly to our faith in the fair play, equal treatment and justice of our government of the United States. . . . As loyal citizens willing to pay the supreme sacrifice for our country, we earnestly plead that certain bans and restrictions be lifted, and that discriminatory rules and regulations imposed upon us as a racial group be dissolved." Coincidentally, the letter was dated March 1, 1944, which was the same day four hundred people at a rally in Heart Mountain in Colorado unanimously declared that men drafted into military service should refuse to report for induction while they were still behind barbed wire.[23]

The first resolution asserted, "Whereas the Selective Service Act states there shall be no discrimination against any person on account of race or color but that the present induction calls for a special combat team composed of Japanese Americans, Be It Resolved that in the future we be given the right to fight side by side with our fellow Caucasian citizens and, Be It Further Resolved that we be given the opportunity and privileges to enlist or volunteer for all branches of the Armed Services without discrimination or segregation."

The last resolution declared that "Whereas certain high-ranking officers of the Armed Forces have made statements attacking the integrity and loyalty of the Japanese Americans, Be It Resolved that all possible efforts be made by the War Department to acquaint these officers with the difference between the enemy and the loyal Japanese Americans."

There is no record of a reply or whether the resolutions were even heard. However, the resolutions' intrinsic value is that the Manzanar prisoners wrote it at all. The meticulous articulation of what must have been hours of private contemplation and lively discussion, coupled with the formalization of their concerns into resolutions, underscores the gravity of their beliefs and purity of their principles. Therefore be it finally resolved that the "Resolutions to the War Department from Delegates of Manzanar Draft Age Citizens" are hereby heard, at last respected and ultimately prized.

### Recovering from History

The intertwining of the notions of recovering history and recovering *from* it suggests that history is a personal concern, that history matters, that our past helps make sense of the present and together impacts the future, and that there is a collectivity of experience that turns "me" and "mine" into "us" and "ours" and makes us responsible for each other.

One incident of historical recovery was intensely personal for me. My biological mother died in 1949, when I was eighteen months old. While I was curating the exhibition, my aunt gave me a box of my mother's personal belongings. Apart from my aunts and uncles, these few possessions and others my aunt has given me over the years are my only links to who my mother was and what gave her life meaning. Among these precious items I found a letter my mother wrote to the Women's Army Auxiliary Corps on November 30, 1942.[24] In it, she expressed her desire to join the WAACs. I was shocked. As one who would never serve in the military, I was chagrined to discover that my mother not only would but actively requested to do so—and while incarcerated in an American concentration camp, at that. I shuffled through the remaining papers, searching for a reply. I found a government response dated December 8, 1942: "At the present time the War Department policy is that, except as may be specifically authorized in exceptional cases, the War Department will not accept for service with the armed forces, Japanese or persons of Japanese extraction, regardless of citizenship status or other factors."[25]

My dismay at finding out that my mother would volunteer to serve in the WAACS turned to indignation that her offer—while completely opposite from my own beliefs—had been rejected. Now angry, I found yet another letter from her to the WAACS, dated January 29, 1943. She wrote, "Since the War Department announced today that plans have been completed for the admission of a substantial number of American citizens of Japanese ancestry to the Army of the United States, I am again writing to request details with regard to induction in the Womens' Army Auxiliary Corps."[26] She received a letter dated a mere three days later, February 1, 1943, from the adjutant general of the War Department, who summarily wrote, "Women of Japanese ancestry are not being enrolled in the Corps. Your desire to serve this country in the Womens' Army Auxiliary Corps is appreciated by the War Department, and it is regretted that you do not meet the eligibility requirements."[27] He also returned her letter. What little I knew about my mother now included the newfound awareness that we would have been entirely at odds on this issue. I also knew that a year later, the Selective Service would reprimand the mothers of Minidoka by stating that military service was not only a duty but a privilege. But as disconcerting as this was, my outrage was entirely overridden by the fact that my mother was rejected, once again, by the government that had abandoned her, one she nevertheless still wanted to serve. I could sense the dejection she must have felt. I took it personally.

### Survival: The Ultimate Resistance

In addition to conducting formal docent training, I had informal discussions with docents and other museum volunteers throughout the development of the exhibition. My purpose was not only to keep them apprised but also, more important, to learn of their insights and experiences as the exhibition planning progressed.

One woman with whom I spoke was eleven when Pearl Harbor was bombed. Her father had died four months earlier and her mother was left with three young children and a boardinghouse. When they were forced into camp, her mother sold the boardinghouse and most of its furnishings for a mere three hundred dollars. Her older brother, now the man of the house at age sixteen, chose her to hold on to all the money they had. Despite the burden of this responsibility, she was honored that her older brother felt he could entrust her with the family's life savings. Before leaving for camp, she sewed a knapsack in which to keep the money. For over two years—she knew the exact length of time to the day—and without ever telling a soul, this little girl carried her family's fortune, the culmination of over thirty years of her parents' hard work, on her back, taking off the knapsack only when she showered and when her mother or brother needed to use some of the money.

I wanted to use this story in the exhibition. It was a resounding account of the enduring intersection between history and real life. She even had the worn knapsack, which she kept for the past fifty years. It would be a disarmingly humble artifact with a heroic story. However, soon after we talked, she came in and patiently explained that when she told her brother about my wanting to use their story, he declined. He gave no objective reason; his unwillingness was reason enough.

Even though they had done nothing wrong, even though it was long ago, she could not convince him to release this memory and share it with others. She told me that if it were up to her and if I thought her experience was worth telling, she would be willing to have the story be known, for she knew how important it was that younger generations understand the event as best they could. But, she said that her brother was of an older generation and set in his ways; after all he had done for her, taking on the responsibility of the family and all, she wanted to honor his feelings and hoped I would as well. Moreover, her brother counseled her that if she were asked any further questions about camp life, she should answer, "I forgot."

I saw a T-shirt recently that declared, "You have the right not to remain silent." I take to heart Pastor Martin Niemoller's well-known warning that if I do not speak out, by the time "they" come for me there will be no one left to speak up. However, this example of the woman's brother and the fact that he had not yet recovered from history illustrates that, where survival is the ultimate resistance, we must also uphold the right to remain silent. And, in addition to silence, forgetting in an unequal world is also a method of survival. In our exalted efforts to recover history, to educate others, and to redefine ourselves, who would deny this man his right to silence? This is not the first story to go untold. I just happened to be present at the right moment to hear it "through the cracks." I relay it here in anonymity because it is so instructive.

## The Ambiguity of Silence

The story of the woman and her brother calls attention to the need to reconsider the role and function of silence. It illustrates the importance of perspective in the study of history and culture and how the perspective of those who experience an event can be so different from that of those who seek to present it. It underscores the limitations of scholarship and presentation and reminds us that in our zeal to know it all, there are things that will never be known. In our eagerness to recover history, we must not only accept that many stories will go untold, we must also understand that that is the way it sometimes must be. It teaches us that silence has a function and role in history.

One viewer criticized the exhibition for being too "silent." Writing in the comment book, he expressed his frustration as a viewer and as a descendant of former inmates: "The artifacts are silent . . . the video is silent. . . . My family has been silent about this whole experience for so long." The historian David Yoo also observed the presence of silence in the exhibition but felt that "silence is a fitting theme since many visitors still lack the words to express their perspectives."[28] And yet, as the educator-activist Alan Nishio warned in a seminal article in 1969, "A time comes when silence is betrayal."[29]

For Japanese Americans, silence has always been an ambiguous zone. Having more than one meaning and being interpreted in divergent ways, our silence has created uncertainty in some, confusion for others, and yet solace and serenity for many. The visitors' lack of words that Yoo mentions regarding the camp experience is the result of many factors: the conflicted space that camp has occupied for us, Japanese American cultural values that are at odds with the values of a Eurocentric society, and our being a "minority" within an American democracy in which some people have too often been deemed more equal than others.

With regard to the camp experience, silence is as much a result of being silenced as choosing to remain silent. The story of the brother who refused to allow his family's story to be told exemplifies the precarious crossroads between the two. It can be said that rather than choosing to forget, the woman's brother was not allowed to remember. Any number of factors—the stifling effect of being victimized, the propaganda that insisted it was our patriotic duty to be detained, the euphemisms designed to hide the truth, the humiliation of having been imprisoned by our own government, the psychological chaos such ironies created—have worked to keep us quiet. While forgetting may be a method of survival, silencing is a method of control.

With respect to Japanese American culture, in adapting traditional Confucian-based values, Issei taught Nisei who taught Sansei to be *otonashii* (respectful, polite), to *gaman* (persevere), and to *enryo* (think more about the well-being of others than the desires of the self). We grew up in a community where to be loud and aggressive is to be uncivil and rude, and good leaders lead by example, not by words. These values become dissonant when we reside in a mainstream society where to be quiet is mistaken for meekness and there are more words than deeds.

Living in a Eurocentric society, in which we are a so-called minority, we are repressed by virtue of falling short of what the poet Audre Lorde called the mythical norm of being "white, thin, male, young, heterosexual, Christian and financially secure."[30] In this country, where equality, freedom, and justice are so vehemently touted, there is a stark contrast between the promise and the reality. Despite the guarantee of freedom of speech, there are unsaid rules that dictate who speaks and who is heard. While some are urged to "speak your mind," others are admonished to "hold your tongue" and "know your place." For Japanese Americans, it has meant being the "model minority," the "quiet Americans."[31]

The artist and critic Coco Fusco writes that "resistance within a colonial context is rarely direct, overt or literal."[32] With regard to the camps, there were many instances of indirect, covert resistance. Bob Uragami, a museum volunteer and close friend, tells the story of his father, a Boy Scout leader, who brought his drum-and-bugle corps to help send off Nisei men from Amache who volunteered for the army.

Eiji Uragami at Heart Mountain. Collection of JANM, gift of Robert and Rumi Uragami (99.2.8B).

The Nisei were transported from the local town's train station in the wee hours of the morning in order to minimize the fact that they volunteered from an American concentration camp. In order to publicize that fact, however, the elder Uragami would have his corps members dress in their formal Boy Scout attire and play as loudly as they could so the whole town would be awakened and know the men were going off to fight the war.[33] This act was not overtly defiant; it couldn't be. But Uragami made his point. He voiced his resistance with drums and bugles and the authorities never even knew it.

## The Struggle of Memory against Forgetting

The exhibition strategy of visitor engagement should be seen not only in terms of partaking and communion, but also in light of the hermeneutic mix of betrayal, cover-up, mixed emotions, and untold stories. The reclamations the exhibition generated are testimony to the persistence of memory in the face of wanting to forget. As Larry Nakashima, one of the volunteers who helped bring the barracks from Wyoming, said, "None of us want to be reminded of it. But the memories we like the least may be the ones that are the most important."[34]

After the successful effort to maintain the integrity of the exhibition at Ellis Island in 1998, I wrote,

> We are at a critical point in the history of the world. In the next millennium there will be no more eyewitnesses to the mistakes of the past. And it will not be left to my generation but to our children and their children to remember—or to forget, to speak out—or to remain silent. The truth is often hard to face, but when 120,000 innocent men, women and children were forced into domestic concentration camps, the power of the Constitution to protect its citizens was weakened for everyone. No matter how difficult, an enduring promise of America is that it is able to confront the truth, admit its wrongs and seek to heal. How can we hope for a better future if we are not willing to face and learn from the past?[35]

The concept of recovering the camp experience and recovering *from* it suggests the larger issue of the infusion of power relationships in history. The historian Michael Frisch discusses the complexity of power and privilege in relationship to the reasons Americans seem to have an uncertain relationship to their history. He relates a conversation with a Nigerian friend, who observed, "You don't need history. What you need is something more like a pretty carpet . . . to cover all those bloodstains on the stairs."[36] While we need to keep vigilant over human rights, we must turn that same watchfulness inward in order to maintain, or regain, sovereignty over ourselves. Racism takes a toll on the human psyche and spirit. As much as we want to educate others, we may need to deprogram ourselves more. We must learn not to apologize when no apology is needed.

This book considers not just the matter of hidden histories and cover-ups but also the ominous question of what becomes history and from whose point of view. Besides being about camp, the exhibition was an exercise in the study and presentation of history and culture. It examined the contrast and connectedness between official history and community memory as well as between the political and the personal. The author Milan Kundera wrote, "The struggle of man against power is the struggle of memory against forgetting."[37] In the course of this prolonged meditation, I discovered that the dual act of recovering necessitates private and public mediation between remembering and forgetting, speaking out and being silent.

Centering the exhibition around the inmates' direct experience and recollections meant that I needed to listen to and appreciate the survivors' anecdotal stories as both authentic and emblematic. Despite my curatorial mission to recover history, I had to avoid the error of denying the inmates' authority and experience in favor of a politicized construction. And despite my desire as a Sansei to expose the injustice of the event, I needed to acknowledge that many Nisei recall camp days with nostalgia. In order to make the exhibition meaningful for them, I had to start where they were—which was, and still is, on a continuum from denial to outrage, from comprehension to acceptance—and be quiet enough to allow their voices to be heard.

Remember the little boy who saw his grandmother's photo in the exhibition and exclaimed that she was part of history? Well, if Grandma is part of history, then I must be, also. And if I am, you are, as well. Just as the visitors to the exhibition were not passive viewers, neither are we. With Grandma, you, and me, we are a multitude, multivocal, with a shared but not singular past. While we may not have been at the epicenter of events, the ripples created by history influence who we are and what we do. America's concentration camps are part of our inheritance—as Japanese Americans, as Americans, as people of conscience. Understanding that doesn't mean having to be loud. Rather we must first be quiet, in order for memory to triumph over forgetting.

# Notes

## Chapter 1: The Legacy of Camp

1. Karen L. Ishizuka, "From the Curator of 'America's Concentration Camps: Remembering the Japanese American Experience,'" *Japanese American National Museum Quarterly* 9, no. 3 (October–December 1994): 2.

2. Commission on Wartime Relocation and Internment of Civilians, *Personal Justice Denied: Report of the Commission on Wartime Relocation and Internment of Civilians* (Washington D.C.: Government Printing Office, 1982), 18.

3. Roy Rosenzweig and David Thelen, "History in Black and Red: African Americans and American Indians and Their Collective Pasts," in *The Presence of the Past: Popular Uses of History in American Life* (New York: Columbia University Press, 1998), 147–76.

4. Quoted in Michi Weglyn, *Years of Infamy: The Untold Story of America's Concentration Camps* (New York: Morrow, 1976), 33–55.

5. For further reading, see C. Harvey Gardiner, *Pawns in a Triangle of Hate: The Peruvian Japanese and the United States* (Seattle: University of Washington Press, 1981), and Seiichi Higashide, *Adios to Tears: The Memoirs of a Japanese Peruvian Internee in U.S. Concentration Camps* (Seattle: University of Washington, 2000).

6. Roger Daniels, introduction to part 6, "Effects of Incarceration Analyzed," in *Japanese Americans: From Relocation to Redress,* ed. Roger Daniels, Sandra C. Taylor, and Harry H. L. Kitano (Seattle: University of Washington Press, 1991), 149.

7. White House Memorandum from President Franklin D. Roosevelt to the Chief of [Naval] Operations, August 10, 1936, National Archives.

8. See, for example, Peter Irons, *Justice at War: The Story of the Japanese American Internment Cases* (New York: Oxford University Press, 1983), 20; Ronald Takaki, *Strangers from a Different Shore* (Boston: Little, Brown, 1989), 390; and Gary Y. Okihiro, *Cane Fires: The Anti-Japanese Movement in Hawaii 1865–1945* (Philadelphia: Temple University Press, 1991), 173–74.

9. Greg Robinson, *By Order of the President: FDR and the Internment of Japanese Americans* (Cambridge, Mass.: Harvard University Press, 2001), 57.

10. See, for example, Alexander H. Leighton, *The Governing of Men: General Principles and Recommendations Based on Experience at a Japanese Relocation Camp*

(1945; Princeton: Princeton University Press, 1968); Jacobus tenBroek, Edward N. Barnhart, and Floyd W. Matson, *Prejudice, War, and the Constitution* (1954; Berkeley: University of California Press, 1975); and Audrie Girdner and Anne Loftis, *The Great Betrayal: The Evacuation of the Japanese Americans during World War II* (London: Macmillan, 1969).

11. John Rankin, *Congressional Record,* December 15, 1941, quoted in tenBroek, Barnhart, and Matson, *Prejudice,* 87.

12. Quoted in Weglyn, *Years of Infamy,* 314.

13. For a typical exclusion order issued by the Western Defense Command and Fourth Army, Wartime Civil Control Administration, see the order illustrated in chapter 4. For more information, see U.S. Department of War, *Final Report: Japanese Evacuation from the West Coast, 1942* (Washington, D.C.: Government Printing Office, 1943), 97–100.

14. War Relocation Authority, *Questions and Answers for Evacuees: Information Regarding the Relocation Program* (San Francisco: War Relocation Authority, Regional office, n.d.).

15. Quoted in Raymond Y. Okamura, "The American Concentration Camps: A Cover-Up through Euphemistic Terminology," *Journal of Ethnic Studies* 10, no. 3 (Fall 1982): 102.

16. Quoted in Merle Miller, *Plain Speaking: An Oral Biography of Harry S. Truman* (New York: Berkeley Publishing Group, 1974), 421.

17. Quoted in Weglyn, *Years of Infamy,* 114.

18. Amy Iwasaki Mass, "Socio-Psychological Effects of the Concentration Camp Experience on Japanese Americans," *Bridge: An Asian American Perspective* (Winter 1978): 61–63.

19. See Raymond Okamura, "Background and History of the Repeal Campaign," *Amerasia Journal* 2, no. 2 (Fall 1974): 73–94.

20. Okamura, "The American Concentration Camps," 104.

21. Editorial, *Los Angeles Times,* May 19, 1942.

22. "Here Are Results of Jap Questionnaire" and "Highlights of Comments in Jap Poll," *Los Angeles Times,* December 6, 1943.

23. Memorandum to National Museum staff from Irene Hirano, Japanese American National Museum, April 6, 1994.

24. Memorandum to Karen Ishizuka from Ralph Appelbaum, Ralph Appelbaum Associates, March 1, 1994.

25. James Hirabayashi, "'Concentration Camp' or 'Relocation Center': What's in a Name?" in special issue on America's Concentration Camps: Remembering the Japanese American Experience, *Japanese American National Museum Quarterly* 9, no. 3 (October–December 1994): 5–10.

26. Memo to Karen Ishizuka and Irene Hirano from James Hirabayashi, March 21, 1994.

27. Notation to Karen Ishizuka on draft of exhibition script from Roger Daniels, July 1994.

28. See Roger Daniels, "The Internment of Japanese Nationals in the United States during World War II," *Halcyon, 1995: A Journal of the Humanities* 17 (1995):

65–75, and memorandum to Karen Ishizuka from Aiko Herzig-Yoshinaga on euphemistic terminology, July 26, 1997.

29. Quoted in Daniels, "Internment of Japanese Nationals," 66.

30. Ibid., 67.

31. John Kuo Wei Tchen, "Creating a Dialogic Museum: The Chinatown History Museum Experiment," in *Museums and Communities: The Politics of Public Culture,* ed. Ivan Karp, Christine Mullen Kreamer, and Steven D. Lavine (Washington, D.C.: Smithsonian Institution, 1992), 291–93.

32. These and other collections are housed at the Japanese American National Museum, Los Angeles.

33. *Through Our Own Eyes* received an Award of Merit from the Chicago International Film Festival (1992) and *Moving Memories* earned a CINE Golden Eagle (1995) and an award from the American Association of State and Local History (1994). *Moving Memories* is available on VHS for purchase from the Japanese American National Museum Store, www.janmstore.com.

## Chapter 2: A Strategy of Process and Participation

1. Harukichi Nakamura was born on December 4, 1908, in Kagoshima, Japan, and passed away on September 24, 2000. Although the Immigration Act of 1924 stopped immigration from Japan, on September 30, 1925, Nakamura, then age seventeen, jumped ship in San Francisco. He forfeited the $500 bond he was required to post to prevent illegal immigration, met his brother in a parking lot, and headed for Los Angeles. He married Kimiko Nitao on October 5, 1932. Having attained the rank of third-degree black belt in judo, he opened the Uwamachi Judo Dojo. He and his wife then opened a small produce market, which they lost when they were sent to Manzanar, California. After the war they settled in Denver, where his brother was living, before returning to Los Angeles in 1946, where Nakamura worked as a gardener until he retired at the age of eighty-four. Besides his two sons, Nakamura had two grandchildren.

2. Kinuko Ito was born August 9, 1898, in Hiroshima, Japan, and passed away on May 21, 1998. She immigrated to Alaska in 1917 before settling in Los Angeles. She was married first to Tokunosuke Tanaka and subsequently to Kumayuki Ito, with whom she went to camp with her two daughters, Tokiko Ann and Mae Yuriko. Another daughter, Rosemary Shizuko, had already married and was sent to another camp. In addition to her three daughters, Ito had ten grandchildren, fourteen great-grandchildren, and four great-great-grandchildren.

3. As indicated in chapter 1, the U.S. government couched the incarceration in euphemistic terms. "An 'assembly center' was a euphemism for a prison." Judge Owen J. Roberts, December 1944, quoted in Okamura, "The American Concentration Camps," 102.

4. This act reflects the assertion of Jay Winter and Emmanuel Sivan that the growth of museums at the end of the twentieth century is a reflection of the business of passing memory from grandparents to grandchildren. See Jay Winter and Emmanuel Sivan, eds., *War and Remembrance in the Twentieth Century* (Cambridge: University Press, 1999), 3.

5. Dolores Hayden, "Landscapes of Loss and Remembrance: The Case of Little Tokyo in Los Angeles," in Winter and Sivan, *War and Remembrance,* 155.

6. Ibid., 153.

7. In an attempt to test the loyalty of incarcerated Japanese Americans, two questionnaires were issued—one by the War Department, to determine who would be eligible for service, and the other by the War Relocation Authority, ostensibly for people who might be released from the camps. Both were referred to as the loyalty questionnaire because each contained question 27, which asked in slightly varying words, "Are you willing to serve in the armed forces of the United States on combat duty, wherever ordered?" and question 28, which asked, also with slightly varying wording, "Will you swear unqualified allegiance to the United States of America and faithfully defend the United States from any and all attack by foreign or domestic forces, and foreswear any form of allegiance to the Japanese Emperor or any other foreign government, power, or organization?" Those who answered no to either or both were designated as "disloyal." Hence, a "no-no" family or person was one that answered no to both questions.

8. Rachel Naomi Remen, *Kitchen Table Wisdom: Stories That Heal* (New York: Riverhead Books, 1996), xxv.

9. Because California was the principal site of the anti-Japanese movement of the early 1920s, California was the first but not only state to enact Alien Land Laws. Washington and Texas soon followed suit. The state of Washington did not repeal its Alien Land Law until 1966. For more information, see Roger Daniels, *The Politics of Prejudice* (New York: Atheneum, 1972).

10. "Woman Seeks Late Mother's Former Helper," *Rafu Shimpo,* October 24, 1995, 3.

11. Personal conversations with Joanne Gertzman, 1995–2005.

12. Lon Yuki Kurashige, "America's Concentration Camps: Remembering the Japanese American Experience," *Journal of American History* 83, no. 1 (June 1996): 161.

13. Matthew Potteiger and Jamie Purinton, *Landscape Narratives: Design Practices for Telling Stories* (New York: Wiley, 1988), 197.

14. David K. Yoo, "Captivating Memories: Museology, Concentration Camps, and Japanese American History," *American Quarterly* 48, no. 4 (December 1996): 688–90.

### Chapter 3: Grandma as History

1. See *Japanese American National Museum Quarterly* 9, no. 3 (October–November 1994).

2. Telephone conversation with Yuki Tamura Yamamoto.

3. Listed on the exhibition acknowledgments panel were volunteers who took back and rebuilt the barracks. They included: Kenji Arai, Sid Arase, Jess Carrera, Nancy Castillo, Joel Castillo, Sharon Yamato Danley, John S. Dietrich, Ethan Etnyre, Ike Fujishin, Mich Fujishin, Jill Fujiwara, Mark Fujiwara, Rodney Fujiwara, Ruby Fujiwara, Sig Fujiwara, Tom Furushiro, Austin Gerken, June Ha-

nashiro, Myles Hanashiro, Ike Hatchimonji, Mike Hatchimonji, Mike Hayashi, Tom Hide, Stan Honda, Joanne Hong, Rich Hong, Kaz Hosozawa, Shunji Hosozawa, Keiichi Ikeda, George Iseri, Joyce Ishizue, Seiso Ishizue, Ryan Kearns, Hal Keimi, Ted Kobara, Katherine Kobayashi, Mitch Maki, Darryl Mikuni, Gary Mikuni, Karen Mikuni, Sam F. Nakamoto, Cayleen Nakamura, Emi Nakashima, Larry Nakashima, Chuck Nishiyama, Harry Nitake, Kiyoshi Noto, Bob Ogawa, Mamoru George Ogi, Mary Ogi, Tosh Ohara, Michael G. Okamura, David Okaya, Shizuko Okumura, Susan Reichert, Carlos Rodriguez, Doug Sagara, Jeff Sakata, Suzanne Sakata, Bacon Sakatani, Kats Sakatani, Mary Sakatani, Sus Satow, Neil Sugimoto, Diane Suzuki, Tommy Takahashi, Kevin Takamiya, Marsha Takamiya, Buddy Takata, Takashi Takemoto, Mickey Takeshita, Nobi Tanigawa, Sharon Tanihara, Aki Tanimoto, Kevin Tokunaga, Mason Ung, Wally Uyehara, Pat Van Der Veer, Jim Yamaguchi, Kimi Yamato, Ron Yamato, Stacy Yamato, Steve Yamato, Susan Yamato, Jack Yee, Charlene Yonai, and Philip M. Yonai.

4. See Sharon Yamato, *Moving Walls: Preserving the Barracks of America's Concentration Camps* (Los Angeles: By the author, 1998).

5. Sharon Yamato Danley, "Project Helps Woman Tear Down a Wall of Silence," *Los Angeles Times,* October 27, 1994.

6. Quoted in Michael Milstein, "Japanese Americans Revisit Their Painful Past," *Los Angeles Times,* October 3, 1994.

7. Stan Honda, "The Heartbeat of Heart Mountain," *San Diego Union Tribune,* November 10, 1994.

8. The following people were docents for the original exhibition at the Japanese American National Museum, from November 1994 to October 1995: Esther Abe, Yae Aihara, Beverly Amano, May Cambra, Pauline Carrillo, Phil Crouch, Its Endo, Miyo Eshita, Sam Fujikawa, Ellen Fujiwara, Kit Fujiwara, Nahan Gluck, Helen Grey, Harue Hamasaki, Nagi Hashiba, Grace Hatae, Ike and Ruth Hatchimonji, Tom Hide, Mary Higashi, Alice Hirata, Fred Hoshiyama, Brian Ikenaga, Joe and Kay Imai, Joyce Inouye, Ayako Iri, Yae Ishii, Sawae Iwamoto, Sumi Iwasaki, Janet Izuno, Eric Kageyama, Craig Kakuda, Jack and Yuki Kanegaye, Stogie Kanogawa, Babe and Mary Karasawa, George and Mary Karatsu, Hal and Barbara Keimi, Jane Kim, Kazuko Kinoshita, Ken Kishiyama, Ben Kitagawa, Ruthie Kitagawa, Brian Kiyabu, Herb and June Kiyabu, Thomas Koiso, Ken Kubota, Mary Kunisaki-Yasui, Frances Kurata, Joyce Kuruma, Eddy Kurushima, Toshiko Kusumoto, Fumi Kuwabara, Doris Lane, Jeff Lane, Howard and Roxana Lewis, Masako Lucraft, Sachi Maehara, Ann Masuda, Marie Masumoto, David and Margaret Masuoka, Nancy Matsuda, Eileen Matsumoto, Mas Matsumoto, Evann Matsumura, Shizu Matsumura, Erik Matsunaga, Sam Mibu, Monte Minami, Kimiyo Miura, Ray and Suzie Miyamoto, Sheri Miyamoto, Midori Miyaoka, Fumi Mochizuki, Darryl Mori, Fumi and Walter Moriya, Masako Koga Murakami, Richard Murakami, Thomas Nakahara, Carol Nakamura, Don Nishida, Shari Oba, Bob Ogawa, Kikko Okada, Kazue Okamura, Mike Okamura, Michi Okano, M. Sid and Yuki Okazaki, Julie Okazaki, Misa Okino, Mas Okui, Ida Onishi, Kimiko Oriba, Chris Oshima, Mary Oye, Lois and Elman Padilla, Bacon Sakatani, Yoshiko Sakurai, Lee Salo, Hitoshi Sameshima, Jennifer

Sato, Brandon Shigeta, Helen Shigetomi, Kiyo Shimamura, Mitz Shiozaki, Bill Shishima, Tak and Helen Shishino, Dorothy Shundo, Sadako Sogioka, Gary Suzuki, Ann Tachikawa, Susan Taira, Lucy Takeuchi, Frank Tanaka, Tadd and Lili Tokuda, Toni Tomita, Jim Tsuda, Isamu Ujiiye, Mits Usui, Mat Uyeno, Grace Maruki Wertz, Toshiko Wiggins, Tom Wong, Tom Yamada, Jogi and Jean Yamaguchi, Kenji Yamamoto, Kunio Yamamoto, Dean Yamanaka, Ken Yamauchi, Herb Yamazaki, Henry and Helen Yasuda, Alayne Yonemoto, Donna Yoshida, Teruyo Yoshimura. There were also community docents at each of the venues of the traveling version of the exhibition.

9. Daniels, *The Politics of Prejudice,* 1.

10. F. R. Brooks, letter to the editor, *Stockton Record,* February 25, 1947.

### Chapter 5: *Something Strong Within*

1. John Esaki, listing for Robert Akira Nakamura in *Encyclopedia of Japanese American History: An A-Z Reference from 1868 to the Present,* updated edition, ed. Brian Niiya (New York: Facts on File, 2001), 291–92 (quote, 291).

2. Unless noted otherwise, this and other remarks by Robert A. Nakamura in this section are from a taped interview with him.

3. Esaki, Nakamura listing, *Encyclopedia of Japanese American History,* 291–92.

4. The author was appointed by the Librarian of Congress to serve on the National Film Preservation Board, 1997–2005.

5. *Through Our Own Eyes* (1990) is a three-screen laser-disc installation directed by Robert A. Nakamura and produced and written by Karen L. Ishizuka for the Japanese American National Museum. It consists of home movies taken by Japanese immigrants in the late 1920s and 1930s as they made the United States their home; the music track comes from 78 rpm records of the era.

6. A longer version of this essay by Robert Rosen will appear in *Mining the Home Movie: Excavations in Histories and Memories,* edited by Karen L. Ishizuka and Patricia Zimmermann, forthcoming from the University of California Press.

7. This review by Joy Yamauchi of *Something Strong Within* appeared in the *Tozai Times,* December 1994. It appears here with permission of the author.

### Chapter 6: Los Japoneses Que Hablan Español and Other Stories That Walked in the Door

1. Daisuke Kitagawa's remark comes from his *Issei and Nisei: The Internment Years* (New York: Seabury Press, 1967), 94.

2. I thank Rha and Kimberly Nickerson for allowing the reprinting of this excerpt from their interview with Emma Perkins and for sharing their late mother's story. Thanks also to Alison Kochiyama for transcribing the interview.

3. Weglyn, *Years of Infamy,* 126.

4. Quoted in Richard Drinnon, *Keeper of Concentration Camps: Dillon S. Myer and American Racism* (Berkeley: University of California Press, 1987), 102.

5. Ibid., 39.

6. Quoted in Leighton, *The Governing of Men,* 104.

7. Thomas K. Walls, *The Japanese Texans* (San Antonio: University of Texas Institute of Texas Cultures, 1987), 188.

8. N. D. Collaer, "The Crystal City Internment Camp," *Department of Justice Immigration and Naturalization Service Monthly Review* 5, no. 6 (December 1947): 77. For more information on Japanese Latin Americans, see Gardiner, *Pawns in a Triangle of Hate;* C. Harvey Gardiner, "The Latin American Japanese and World War II," in Daniels, Taylor, and Kitano, *Japanese Americans,* 142–45; Higashide, *Adios to Tears.*

9. Gutierrez defined a Chicano as a person of Mexican ancestry who is a cultural nationalist and politically active.

10. Maury Maverick, "Memory and Mending Fences," *San Antonio Express News,* December 1, 1985.

11. Rita Nute, "A Real-Life UTA Maverick," *UTA Magazine,* Winter 1994, 13.

## Chapter 7: Coming to Terms

I thank Art Hansen, Irene Hirano, and Lloyd Inui of the Japanese American National Museum for reading and commenting on this chapter. An adaptation was published as "Coming to Terms: America's Concentration Camps," in *Common Ground: The Japanese American National Museum and the Culture of Collaborations,* edited by Akemi Kikumura-Yano, Lane Ryo Hirabayashi, and James A. Hirabayashi (Boulder: University of Colorado Press, 2005), 101–22. Previous versions were presented at "Confronting the Past: Memory, Identity and Society: A Comparative and Cross-Cultural Conference," sponsored by the "1939" Club Holocaust Memorial Fund and the UCLA Center for Jewish Studies, February 2001, Los Angeles, California, and at the American Association of State and Local History Annual Meeting, November 2002, Portland, Oregon.

1. The public program was held on March 29, 1998, at New York University and sponsored by the Japanese American National Museum, the NYU Asian/Pacific/American Studies Program, and the NYU Hebrew and Judaic Studies Program with funding from the Nathan Cummings Foundation. Other speakers included Henry Feingold, Setsuko Nishi, Congressman Norman Mineta, and Jeffrey Shandler; Catherine Stimpson served as moderator. The assessment of Egon Mayer's status comes from Joe Berkofsy, "Demographer Egon Mayer, 59, Advocate of Outreach, Is Dead," Global News Service of the Jewish People, February 2, 2004.

2. "Harbor Camp for Enemy Aliens," *New York Times Magazine,* January 25, 1942, 29.

3. E-mail to Karen Ishizuka from Melanie Ide, Ralph Appelbaum Associates, New York, November 18, 1997.

4. Executive summary by Irene Hirano to the Executive Committee, National Museum Board, staff and volunteers, Japanese American National Museum, January 27, 1998.

5. Facsimile to Karen Ishizuka from Diane Dayson, Superintendent, Statue

of Liberty National Monument, National Park Service, U.S. Department of the Interior, January 20, 1998.

6. Internal memo from Irene Hirano to Karen Ishizuka, Chris Komai, and Cayleen Nakamura, Japanese American National Museum, January 27, 1998.

7. Facsimile to Diane Dayson from Karen Ishizuka, Senior Curator, Japanese American National Museum, January 27, 1998.

8. Facsimile to Irene Hirano from Diane Dayson, February 4, 1998.

9. Facsimile to Irene Hirano and Karen Ishizuka from Dr. Harry Abe, New York Advisory Committee, February 6, 1998.

10. Japanese American National Museum, Los Angeles, telephone log of February 5–6, 1998.

11. E-mail to Karen Ishizuka from Aiko Herzig-Yoshinaga, Virginia, February 6, 1998.

12. Letter to Irene Hirano from Masako and Richard Murakami, Los Angeles, February 11, 1998.

13. Letter to Irene Hirano from Lonnie G. Bunch III, Associate Director for Curatorial Affairs, National Museum of American History, Washington, D.C., February 12, 1998.

14. Letter to Irene Hirano and Karen Ishizuka from Lamont Yeakey, Department of History, California State University, Los Angeles, February 6, 1998.

15. For more information on the redress movement, see Daniels, Taylor, and Kitano, *Japanese Americans;* William Hohri, *Repairing America: An Account of the Movement for Japanese American Redress* (Pullman: Washington State University Press, 1988); and Mitchell T. Maki, Harry H. L. Kitano and S. Megan Berthold, *Achieving the Impossible Dream: How Japanese Americans Obtained Redress* (Urbana: University of Illinois Press, 1999).

16. Japanese American National Museum, Los Angeles, telephone log of February 5–6, 1998.

17. Letter to Karen Ishizuka from Mitchell T. Maki, Assistant Professor, School of Public Policy and Social Research, University of California, Los Angeles, February 4, 1998.

18. Letter to Irene Hirano from Tom L. Freudenheim, Executive Director, Yivo Institute for Jewish Research, New York, February 6, 1998.

19. Letter to Irene Hirano from Egon Mayer, Professor, Department of Sociology, Brooklyn College of the City University of New York, February 11, 1998.

20. Letter to the Honorable Bruce Babbitt, Secretary, Department of the Interior, from Daniel K. Inouye, United States Senate, February 5, 1998.

21. Wong explained that the superintendent of Ellis Island (Diane Dayson) reports to one of five regional directors (Marie Rust), who reports to the assistant secretary for Fish, Wildlife, and Parks (Don Barry), who reports to the deputy secretary (John Garamendi), who reports to the secretary of the interior (Bruce Babbitt).

22. E-mail to Karen Ishizuka from Roger Daniels, Professor, University of Cincinnati, February 6, 1997.

23. Jeffrey Wentraub faxed us the article on February 26, 1998, noting that it appeared that day in about a dozen Jewish newspapers.

24. Somini Sengupta, "What Is a Concentration Camp? Ellis Island Exhibit Prompts a Debate," *New York Times,* March 8, 1998.

25. Mae M. Cheng, "Who Defines 'Concentration Camp'?" *New York Newsday,* March 8, 1998.

26. The attendees were Shula Bahat, American Jewish Committee (AJC); Martin Bresler, AJC's Belfer Center for American Pluralism; Jerome Chanes, National Foundation for Jewish Culture; Guila Franklin, Jewish Council for Public Affairs (JCPA); Jerry Goodman, National Committee for Labor Israel; David Harris, AJC; Irene Hirano, Japanese American National Museum (JANM); Senator Daniel Inouye; Karen L. Ishizuka, JANM; Howie Katz, Anti-Defamation League; Tom Kometani, Japanese American Citizens League (JACL); Bill Lenahan, National Ethnic Coalition of Organizations (NECO); Benjamin Meed, American Gathering of Jewish Holocaust Survivors; Norman Mineta, former congressman; Michael Muller, New York Jewish Community Relations Council; Suki Ports, JANM New York Advisory Council; Martin Raffel, JCPA; Todd Richman, American Jewish Congress; Lawrence Rubin, JCPA; Stephen Steinlight, AJC; Diane Steinman, AJC; Kenneth Stern, AJC; Ron Uba, JACL; and Michi Weglyn, author.

27. Somini Sengupta, "Accord on Term 'Concentration Camp,'" *New York Times,* March 10, 1998; Mae M. Cheng, "Accord Reached on Exhibit Title," *New York Newsday,* March 10, 1998.

28. Editorial, "Words for Suffering," *New York Times,* March 10, 1998.

29. See, for example, "'Concentration Camp' Sparks Debate between Japanese Americans, Jews," *Washington Times,* March 11, 1998.

30. Martin Lapidus, letter to the editor, *Jewish Week,* March 13, 1998.

31. Fred Okrand, letter to the editor, *Jewish Journal of Greater Los Angeles* 14, no. 3 (March 13–19, 1998).

32. "Lagerdenken," *Der Spiegel,* December 1998, 259.

33. Quoted in Weglyn, *Years of Infamy,* 112.

34. Clyde Haberman, "Defending Jews' Lexicon of Anguish," *New York Times,* March 13, 1998.

35. Jonathan Mark, "Passing Judgement," *Jewish Week,* March 13, 1998.

36. John Nishio, letter to the editor, *Pacific Citizen,* May 1–14, 1998.

37. Mas Odoi, letter to the editor, *Pacific Citizen,* May 1–14, 1998.

38. Toru Miyoshi, letter to the editor, *Pacific Citizen,* April 17–30, 1998.

39. Transcription of audio recording, March 29, 1998, public program at New York University.

## Chapter 8: Recovering History and Recovering *from* History

1. Dorothy Swaine Thomas and Richard Nishimoto, *The Spoilage: Japanese American Evacuation and Resettlement* (Berkeley: University of California Press, 1946), 363.

2. Ibid, 369.

3. Ibid, 369–70.

4. Handwritten statement by Joe Kurihara, collection of Japanese American National Museum, gift of Charles and Lois Ferguson (93.3.1).

5. For more information on Minoru Yasui's case and the other cases, see Irons, *Justice at War,* and Peter Irons, ed., *Justice Delayed: The Record of the Japanese American Internment Cases* (Middletown, Conn.: Wesleyan University Press, 1989).

6. "Evacuation," by Minoru Yasui, copied into scrapbook by Masao Yasui, Santa Fe Internment Camp, March 24, 1943, collection of Japanese American National Museum, gift of Kay Takeoka, (93.1.1).

7. Letter to President Franklin D. Roosevelt from the Mothers' Society of Minidoka, February 20, 1944, collection of Japanese American National Museum, gift of Midori Miyaoka (94.55.5).

8. Letter to the Mothers' Society of Minidoka from the Selective Service System, March 14, 1944, collection of Japanese American National Museum, gift of Midori Miyaoka (94.55.6).

9. Letter to Karen Ishizuka from Mamoru Inouye, February 22, 1995.

10. Photocopies of two photographs of Heart Mountain marked "Photo Collections of Yoshio Okumoto."

11. Julia Sommer, "Pre-war Japanese Students Give Scholarship," *Stanford Observer,* November 1987.

12. In the prologue to his book *Keeper of Concentration Camps,* Richard Drinnon wrote that he was given such stones by a homesteader at Heart Mountain. He had the characters translated and surmised that they were "from the dialogues of the Buddha" (xxi).

13. Les and Nora Bovee Collection, Japanese American National Museum (94.158.1)

14. "Heart Mountain Mystery Rocks Donated to Museum," *Japanese American National Museum Quarterly* 1, no. 1 (July–September 1994): 14–15.

15. Letter to the Japanese American National Museum from Shinjiro Kanzawa, April 28, 1999.

16. Letter to Karen Ishizuka from Mary Seko, December 3, 1994.

17. Erica Harth, "Children of Manzanar," *Massachussetts Review* (Fall 1993): 376–91. Harth also wrote a book on the subject, *Last Witnesses: Reflections on the Wartime Internment of Japanese Americans* (New York: Palgrove Press, 2001).

18. Harth, "Children of Manzanar," 372.

19. Ibid., 376.

20. Ibid., 388.

21. Ibid., 390.

22. "Resolutions to the War Department from Delegates of Manzanar Draft Age Citizens," with cover letter to Ralph Merritt, Director, Manzanar, March 1, 1944, Jogi Yamaguchi Collection, Japanese American National Museum (90.20.1a).

23. Niiya, *Encyclopedia of Japanese American History,* 68.

24. Letter to Director, Women's Army Auxiliary Corps, Ft. Des Moines, Iowa,

from Tomiko Karen Okura, Jerome Relocation Center, Denson, Arkansas, November 30, 1942.

25. Letter to Tomiko Karen Okura from War Department, Women's Army Auxiary Corps, Office of the Director, Washington, D.C., December 8, 1942.

26. Letter to Appointment and Induction Branch, Women's Army Auxiliary Corps, Washington, D.C., from Tomiko K. Okura, January 29, 1943.

27. Letter to Tomiko K. Okura from J. A. Ulio, Major General, Office of the Adjutant General, War Department, February 1, 1943.

28. Yoo, "Captivating Memories," 690.

29. Alan Nishio, "The Oriental as 'Middleman Minority,'" *Gidra* 1, no. 2 (May 1969): 3.

30. Audre Lorde, "Age, Race, Class, and Sex: Women Redefining Difference," in *Out There: Marginalization and Contemporary Cultures,* ed. Russell Ferguson, Martha Gever, Trinh T. Minh-ha, and Cornel West (Cambridge, Mass.: MIT Press, 1990), 282.

31. William Petersen used the phrase "model minority" in "Success Story: Japanese American Style," *New York Times Magazine,* January 9, 1966, 20. A similar article, entitled "Success Story: Outwhiting the Whites," appeared in *Newsweek,* June 21, 1971, 24–25. Bill Hosokawa called Japanese Americans "quiet Americans" in his book *Nisei: The Quiet Americans* (New York: William Morrow, 1969).

32. Coco Fusco, *English Is Broken Here: Notes on Cultural Fusion in the Americas* (New York: New Press, 1995), 35.

33. Bob Uragami, personal conversation with author, July 1994.

34. Quoted in Milstein, "Japanese Americans Revisit Their Painful Past."

35. Karen L. Ishizuka, "America's Concentration Camps at Ellis Island," *Rafu Magazine,* May 8, 1998, 9.

36. Michael Frisch, *Shared Authority* (Albany: State University of New York Press, 1989), 20.

37. Milan Kundera, *The Book of Laughter and Forgetting* (New York: Harper Perennial, 1994), 4. I thank Saachiko Takita for bringing this statement to my attention.

# Selected Readings

Armor, John, and Peter Wright. *Manzanar.* New York: Times Books, 1988.

Austin, Allan W. *From Concentration Camp to Campus: Japanese American Students and World War II.* Urbana: University of Illinois Press, 2004.

Bosworth, Allan R. *America's Concentration Camps.* New York: Norton, 1967.

Commission on Wartime Relocation and Internment of Civilians. *Personal Justice Denied: Report of the Commission on Wartime Relocation and Internment of Civilians.* Washington, D.C.: Government Printing Office, 1982.

Daniels, Roger. *Concentration Camps USA.* New York: Holt, Rinehart, and Winston, 1971.

———. "The Internment of Japanese Nationals in the United States during World War II." *Halcyon, 1995: A Journal of the Humanities* 17 (1995): 65–75.

———. *Prisoners without Trial: Japanese Americans in World War II.* 2nd ed. New York: Hill and Wang, 2004.

———. "Words Do Matter: A Note on Inappropriate Terminology and the Incarceration of the Japanese Americans." In *Nikkei in the Pacific Northwest: Japanese Americans and Japanese Canadians in the Twentieth Century,* ed. Louis Fiset and Gail Nomura, 183–207. Seattle: University of Washington Press, 2005.

Daniels, Roger, Sandra C. Taylor, and Harry H. L. Kitano, eds. *Japanese Americans: From Relocation to Redress.* Salt Lake City: University of Utah Press, 1986

Drinnon, Richard. *Keeper of Concentration Camps: Dillon S. Myer and American Racism.* Berkeley: University of California Press, 1987.

Duus, Masayo. *Unlikely Liberators: The Men of the 100th and the 442nd.* Honolulu: University of Hawai'i Press, 1987.

Fiset, Louis. *Imprisoned Apart: The World War II Correspondence of an Issei Couple.* Seattle: University of Washington Press, 1997.

Gardiner, C. Harvey. *Pawns in a Triangle of Hate: The Peruvian Japanese and the United States.* Seattle: University of Washington Press, 1981.

Gensensway, Deborah, and Mindy Roseman. *Beyond Words: Images from America's Concentration Camps.* Ithaca: Cornell University Press, 1987.

Harth, Erica. *Last Witnesses: Reflections on the Wartime Internment of Japanese Americans.* New York: Palgrove Press, 2001.

Higa, Karin M., ed. *The View from Within: Japanese American Art from the Internment Camps, 1942–1945.* Los Angeles: UCLA Wight Art Gallery and the UCLA Asian American Studies Center, 1992.

Higashide, Seiichi. *Adios to Tears: The Memoirs of a Japanese Peruvian in U.S. Concentration Camps.* Seattle: University of Washington Press, 2000.

Hill, Kimi Kodani, ed. *Topaz Moon: Chiura Obata's Art of the Internment.* Berkeley, Calif.: Heydey Books, 2000.

Hohri, William. *Repairing America: An Account of the Movement for Japanese American Redress.* Pullman: Washington State University Press, 1988.

Ichioka, Yuji, ed. *Views from Within: The Japanese American Evacuation and Resettlement Study.* Los Angeles: UCLA Asian American Studies Center, 1989.

Inada, Lawson Fusao, ed. *Only What We Could Carry: The Japanese American Internment Experience.* Berkeley, Calif.: Heydey Books, 2000.

Irons, Peter. *Justice at War: The Story of the Japanese American Internment Cases.* New York: Oxford University Press, 1983.

———, ed. *Justice Delayed: The Record of the Japanese American Internment Cases.* Middletown, Conn.: Wesleyan University Press, 1989.

Japanese American National Museum. Chronology and other resources. www.janm.org/nrc/resources.php.

Kitagawa, Daisuke. *Issei and Nisei: The Internment Years.* New York: Seabury Press, 1967.

Leighton, Alexander. *The Governing of Men: General Principles and Recommendations Based on Experience at a Japanese Relocation Camp.* Princeton: Princeton University Press, 1968.

Maki, Mitchell, Harry H. L. Kitano, and S. Megan Berthold. *Achieving the Impossible Dream: How Japanese Americans Obtained Redress.* Urbana: University of Illinois Press, 1999.

Nakano, Jiro, and Kay Nakano, eds. and trans. *Poets behind Barbed Wire.* Honolulu: Bamboo Ridge, 1983.

Niiya, Brian, ed. *Encyclopedia of Japanese American History: An A-to-Z Reference from 1868 to the Present.* Updated edition. New York: Facts on File, 2001.

Okada, John. *No-No Boy.* Seattle: University of Washington Press, 1979.

Okamura, Raymond Y. "The American Concentration Camps: A Cover-Up through Euphemistic Terminology." *Journal of Ethnic Studies* 10, no. 3 (Fall 1982): 95–108.

Okubo, Mine. *Citizen 13660.* Reprint. Seattle: University of Washington Press, 1983.

Robinson, Greg. *By Order of the President: FDR and the Internment of Japanese Americans.* Cambridge, Mass.: Harvard University Press, 2001.

Sone, Monica. *Nisei Daughter.* Reprint. Seattle: University of Washington Press, 1979.

Tateishi, John. *And Justice for All: An Oral History of the Japanese American Detention Camps.* New York: Random House, 1984.

Thomas, Dorothy Swaine, and Richard Nishimoto. *The Spoilage: Japanese American Evacuation and Resettlement.* Berkeley: University of California Press, 1946.

Weglyn, Michi. *Years of Infamy: The Untold Story of America's Concentration Camps.* New York: Morrow, 1976.

Yamamoto, Eric K., et al. *Race, Rights, and Reparation: Law and the Japanese American Internment.* New York: Aspen, 2001.

# Index

Page numbers in italic refer to illustrations

laborers, 150, 151; monument at, 150, 152; as multinational/ethnic segregation and isolation camp, 86, 149; scrip used in, *85;* statistical profile of, *84. See also* Gutierrez, Jose Angel; Leupp Isolation Center

Crystal City Association, 152

Crystal City Country Club, 151

Crystal City school board, 151–52; and Alan Tanaguchi, 152

cultural landscapes, 25–26

CWRIC. *See* Commission on Wartime Relocation and Internment of Civilians

Daniels, Roger, 9; and terminology, 12, 13, 161–62

Danley, Sharon Yamato, 43

Dayson, Diane, 156, 160, 162, 163; and "concentration camp," 156–57; and demand for new exhibit title, 157

*Der Spiegel*, 168, *169*

detention orders, as "civilian exclusion orders," 9. *See also* euphemisms; terminology

discrimination: comparative, 55–56, 122, 147–48; against Japanese Americans, 50–51, 62. *See also* naturalization; segregation

"disloyals," 113, 147. See also *Questions and Answers for Evacuees*

docents, 43, 47, 185–86, 189; badges of, *45, 46, 47, 48, 49;* and ethnic identity, 141–42; as exhibit participants, 43–49; and feedback to curator, 185–86; interactive contributions of, 44–46; training of, 44, 50

the draft: induction at Manzanar, *78;* and irony of induction from camp, 79; speech to draftees, 78; and volunteer from camp, *83. See also* Minidoka, Mothers'

Society of; "Resolutions to the War Department from Delegates of Manzanar Draft Age Citizens"; Selective Service

draft resistance, *91,* 183. *See also* Heart Mountain Fair Play Committee; Urakama, Eiji

Drinnon, Richard, 9; compares treatment of Japanese Americans and Indians, 147–48; and "mystery rocks," 179–80

Eames, Charles and Ray, 123

"Eleven Demands" to War Relocation Authority, *82*

Ellis Island, as detention center, 155

Ellis Island Foundation and exhibit title, 160–61

Ellis Island Immigration Museum, 4, 155, 160, 163, 166

Emergency Detention Act, 10, 164–65

Emi, Frank, 90, *90*

Endo, Masayoshi, Rohwer home movie by, 119

enemy aliens and internment, 13; "basic personnel record," 53

ethnic groups and the camps, 146–49. *See also* American Indians; Caucasians; Chicanos and the camps

ethnic identity, 4

ethnic minorities and discrimination, *62,* 63

euphemisms, 11, *72;* discarding of, 11; function, 10; and Japanese American community, 10. *See also* terminology

European immigrants, 50

evacuation: community and individual, 16; opinions regarding, 54–55

exclusion order, *68*

Executive Order 9066, 7, 51, 70, 71, 174

exhibit. *See* America's Concentration Camps: Remembering the Japanese American Experience

Fair Play Committee (FPC), at Heart Mountain, *90,* 90–91

families: and camp, 19, 67, *83, 85, 106,* 124; and camp births, 22; and depiction of camp meal, *109. See also* barracks; camp albums; Crystal City; *individual camps,* statistical profiles of

FBI, and arrests of Japanese Americans, 51

Ferguson, Charles, *96,* 97

Ferguson, Lois, *96,* 97

Filipino strikers, *63*

FPC. *See* Fair Play Committee

Franklin, Benjamin, and racism, 62

Frederick, Francis S., 147, 148

Freudenheim, Tom, 159–60

Frisch, Michael, 191

Fujii, George Shichitaro, 85. *See also* Fujii family

Fujii family, *85;* autograph book of, *86*

Fusco, Coco, 189

Garamendi, John, 161

German Americans and internment, 19, 60, 70, 122. *See also* discrimination, comparative

Germans, 149

Gertzman, Joanne Grossman, *36;* and search for Toshi Hieshima, 35–37

Gila River (Arizona): panoramic view of, *87;* on reservation land, 147; statistical profile of, 87

Goldberg, J. J., 163

Goodluck, Mary Ann, 146

Grenada Relocation Center, statistical profile of, 81

Grossman family, 35–37, *36. See also* Gertzman, Joanne Grossman

Guadalupe (California), home

movie of forced removal from, 119, *131*, 136

Gutierrez, Jose Angel, 150, 151. *See also* Crystal City

Haberman, Clyde, and appropriation of terms, 168–70

Hamamoto, Jean, 140

Hanami, Clement, 21, 155

Hansen, Arthur, 159

Harris, David, and terminology, 165–66

Harth, Erica, 182–83

Hashizume, Naokichi, and Heart Mountain home movie, 119

Hasuike, Robert, 19

Hatchimonji, Ike, 44–45; portrait and docent badge of, *46*

Hawai'i: and plantation hierarchy, 63; and plantation song, 64; and strike of Japanese and Filipino workers, *63*

Hayashi, Akira and Yoshio, and home movies by, 119

Hayden, Dolores, 25, 26

Hearst newspapers, 11

Heart Mountain (Wyoming), 40, 41, 46, 177; billboard photograph of, *178;* and draft resistance in, 90–91, 183; on exhibit banner, *76;* home movie of, by Naokichi Hashizume, 119; inmate in, *89;* and location on Indian reservation land, 147; and "mystery rocks," 179–81, *181;* reconstruction of barracks in, 40–43, *42;* statistical profile of, 89. *See also* barrack; draft resistance; Fair Play Committee; Okumoto, Yoshio

Heart Mountain Fair Play Committee. *See* Fair Play Committee

*Heart Mountain Sentinel*, 78

Herzig-Yoshinaga, Aiko, 13, 158

Hieshima, Toshi, *36;* the search for, 35–37

Higashi Hongwanji Betsuin, 179

Hirabayashi, Gordon, 116

Hirabayashi, James, 12

Hirabayashi, Lane Ryo, 9

Hirano, Irene, 12, 156, 157, 162, *165*

Hiroshima, 150

Hispanics. *See* Japanese Latin Americans; Japanese Peruvians; Latinos; Mexican Americans

Holocaust: and comparative discrimination, 13, 55, 125; and "concentration camp," 157, 166–68; survivors, 54. *See also* Haberman, Clyde

Holocaust National Museum (Washington, D.C.), 161

home movies, 15, 16, 119–21, *120,* 125, 126; as basis for *Something Strong Within*, 119. *See also* historical memory; *Something Strong Within*

Honda, David, 41

Honda, Stan, 43

Ide, Melanie, *3, 4*

Immigrant Exclusion Act (1924), 51

immigrant rights, 33

immigration, 33; by Japanese and Europeans, 62

Imoto, Mary, 180

incarceration, of Japanese Americans: numbers involved in, 60; possible recurrence of, 30; reasons for, 2, 60, 114–16, 177; and submissiveness, 175, 176, 183–84; as unconstitutional, 60; unfairness of, 174; uniqueness of, 57

Inouye, Daniel K., 160–61, 162, *165;* address by, at Jewish–Japanese American meeting, 164; and Dachau, 164–65

Inouye, Mamuro, 178–79

*Inside an American Concentration Camp* (Nishimoto), 9

internment: as legal term, 13; numbers of Japanese compared to Germans and Italians interned, 60; of Momota Okura and other inmates, *70. See also individual camps;* Justice Department internment camps

interracial marriage, 141

Iseri, George, 41, *42*

Ishizuka, George, *5*

Ishizuka, Henry, *66*

Ishizuka, Karen, *3, 24, 42, 165;* as collector of information and artifacts, 7, 44; and "concentration camp," 156–57, 162, 166, 167; criticism of, 170; and docents and volunteers, 44, 185–86, 189; and ethnic groups involved in camps, 149; and family illustrations, *xix, 5, 52, 53, 64, 66, 67, 70, 94, 96, 150;* and family or personal memories, 64; and home movies, 126; and memory, 190–92; problems of, as curator, 173, 191; and traveling exhibit, 156

Ishizuka family, *5*

isolation camps, 147

Issei: in eyes of Nisei, 30; and internment, 13

Italian Americans, 60, 122; and camps, 19; internment of, 70. *See also* discrimination, comparative

Italians, 149

Ito, Kinuko, 22–23, *24*

Ito, Rinban Noriaki, 179

Iwasaki, Bruce, 161

Japan: deeds of, blamed on Japanese Americans, 56–56; as supplier of relief goods, *82*

Japanese Alaskans, 75

Japanese American Citizens League (JACL), 164. See also *Pacific Citizen*

Japanese American community: and camps, 7; and economic loss,

8; historian members of, 8–9; and search for missing friends, 34–35; and shame, 173; and silence, 188; submissiveness/protest by, 175, 183–84; values of, 189

Japanese American National Museum: criticized, 169–70; design team of, *3;* direct mailing campaign and response, 54–55; and Ellis Island Immigration Museum, 155; foundation and mission of, 3, 12, 13; and terminology, 156, 157–58. *See also* museum staff; New York Advisory Council

*Japanese American National Museum Quarterly,* 180

Japanese Americans: blamed for deeds of Japan, 56; and citizenship, 50; compared to Italians and Germans, 2; as "coolies," 65; and the draft, 77–80, 175, 176–77; internment of, 13; as non-aliens, 9; and proving loyalty, 76; seen as Japanese, 56–57; status of, 2

Japanese Bruins Club, *64*

Japanese Hawaiians, 6, 8; labor strike of, *63;* during World War II, 75

Japanese Latin Americans, 8, 19, 151; at Crystal City, 149; as hostages, 73–74

Japanese Peruvians: interned, 73–74; Girl Scouts, *73*

Japanese Students Association (Stanford University), 179

"Jap Questionnaire," 11

Jerome (Arkansas), 93–94; barracks, *92;* home movies, 119; statistical profile of, 92; Sunday school students in, 93–94. *See also* Hayashi, Akira and Yoshio; Hieshima, Toshi; Gertzman, Joanne Grossman; Watanabe, Gunji

Jewish Community Relations Council (New York), 164

Jewish Council for Public Affairs, 164

Jewish Holocaust. *See* Holocaust

*Jewish Journal,* 168

Jewish newspapers, and terminology, 163

Jewish scholars, and use of "concentration camp," 159–60

*Jewish Week,* 168, 169

Jews and use of "concentration camp," 156; discussed with leaders, 161. *See also* "concentration camp"; Haberman, Clyde

Johnson, Franklin, and home movies by, 119, *119, 131*

Justice Department internment. See Crystal City; internment

Justice Department internment camps, 85, 155; claims, 149; inmates, *70*

Kaji, Bruce, 162

Kanazawa, Chizuyo, 83, *83*

Kanazawa, Shinjiro, 180–81

Kanazawa family, *83*

Katsuko, text of immigrant hopes, 66

Kawamoto, Mitsu, *61*

Kawamoto brother, *61*

*Keeper of Concentration Camps* (Drinnon), 9

Kirshenblatt-Gimblett, Barbara, 14

Kitagawa, Daisuke, 143

Kitagawa, Toshio, 16

Koga, Masako. *See* Murakami, Masako Koga

Kochiyama, Alison, 149

Kochiyama, Yuri Nakahara, *93, 94,* 93–94, 118, 119; and courage, 136

Korematsu, Fred, 116

Krall, Hanna, 26

Kubota, Guntaro, *90*

Kumamoto, Junji, inducted from behind bars, 79

Kuramoto, Dan, 119, 127

Kurashige, Lon Yuki, 37

Kurihara, Joe, 175;

Kuroki, Ben, *132*

labor unions, 51; and discrimination, 62

Lapidus, Martin, 168

Latinos, 33–34

Leupp Isolation Center (Arizona), 148, 175; multiethnic history of, 149; as site of Bureau of Indian Affairs boarding school, 148; video of incarceration about, 146, 147. *See also* American Indian reservations; isolation camps

Little Rock Statehouse Convention Center (Arkansas), 4

Lockard, Ben and Ken, 146

Lockard, Jane, 146; and Nez video project, 148; on treatment of Japanese Americans and Indians, 147–48

Long, Lucion, 148

Lorde, Audre, 188

*Los Angeles Herald Express,* clipping from, *11*

*Los Angeles Times,* 11

"Lost and Found" bulletin board, 34–37

Lowey, Jacqueline, 162–63

Maeshiro, Sandy, 22

Maki, Michael, 159

*Manzanar* (film), 123–24

Manzanar (California), 148, 175; army induction at, *78;* children in, *95, 122;* map and barracks of, 22; Merritt Park garden in, 96; model of, 19; riot in, 97, 175; statistical profile of, 95; student teachers in, *96. See also* Harth, Erica; Manzanar Pilgrimage;

KAREN L. ISHIZUKA is an award-winning media producer whose films related to the World War II experience of Japanese Americans include *Toyo Miyatake: Infinite Shades of Gray* (2001), *Once upon a Camp*, a three-part series for youth (2000), *From Bullets to Ballots* (1997), *Looking Like the Enemy* (1995), *Something Strong Within* (1994), and *Conversations: Before the War/After the War* (1985). She is a former department director, senior producer, and senior curator at the Japanese American National Museum and is the co-editor of *Mining the Home Movie: Excavations into Historical and Cultural Memories* (forthcoming).

*The Asian American Experience*

The Hood River Issei: An Oral History of Japanese Settlers in Oregon's
  Hood River Valley   *Linda Tamura*
Americanization, Acculturation, and Ethnic Identity: The Nisei Generation
  in Hawaii   *Eileen H. Tamura*
Sui Sin Far/Edith Maude Eaton: A Literary Biography   *Annette White-Parks*
Mrs. Spring Fragrance and Other Writings   *Sui Sin Far; edited by Amy Ling
  and Annette White-Parks*
The Golden Mountain: The Autobiography of a Korean Immigrant,
  1895–1960   *Easurk Emsen Charr; edited and with an introduction by
  Wayne Patterson*
Race and Politics: Asian Americans, Latinos, and Whites in a
  Los Angeles Suburb   *Leland T. Saito*
Achieving the Impossible Dream: How Japanese Americans
  Obtained Redress   *Mitchell T. Maki, Harry H. L. Kitano, and
  S. Megan Berthold*
If They Don't Bring Their Women Here: Chinese Female Immigration
  before Exclusion   *George Anthony Peffer*
Growing Up Nisei: Race, Generation, and Culture among Japanese
  Americans of California, 1924–49   *David K. Yoo*
Chinese American Literature since the 1850s   *Xiao-huang Yin*
Pacific Pioneers: Japanese Journeys to America and Hawaii, 1850–80
  *John E. Van Sant*
Holding Up More Than Half the Sky: Chinese Women Garment Workers
  in New York City, 1948–92   *Xiaolan Bao*
Onoto Watanna: The Story of Winnifred Eaton   *Diana Birchall*
Edith and Winnifred Eaton: Chinatown Missions and Japanese
  Romances   *Dominika Ferens*
Being Chinese, Becoming Chinese American   *Shehong Chen*
"A Half Caste" and Other Writings   *Onoto Watanna; edited by
  Linda Trinh Moser and Elizabeth Rooney*
Chinese Immigrants, African Americans, and Racial Anxiety in the
  United States, 1848–82   *Najia Aarim-Heriot*
Not Just Victims: Conversations with Cambodian Community Leaders
  in the United States   *Edited and with an Introduction by Sucheng Chan;
  interviews conducted by Audrey U. Kim*

The University of Illinois Press
is a founding member of the
Association of American University Presses.

---

University of Illinois Press
1325 South Oak Street
Champaign, IL 61820-6903
www.press.uillinois.edu